TO SAVE AND TO DESTROY

The Charles Eliot Norton Lectures, 2023–2024

TO SAVE AND TO DESTROY

WRITING AS AN OTHER

VIET THANH NGUYEN

THE BELKNAP PRESS OF HARVARD UNIVERSITY PRESS

CAMBRIDGE, MASSACHUSETTS

LONDON, ENGLAND

2025

Copyright © 2025 by the President and Fellows of Harvard College

All rights reserved

Printed in the United States of America

First printing

Solmaz Sharif, "Contaminated Remains," from *Look*. Copyright © 2016 by Solmaz Sharif. Reprinted with permission of The Permissions Company, LLC on behalf of Graywolf Press.

Layli Long Soldier, excerpts "Whereas Statements" from *Whereas*. Copyright © 2017 by Layli Long Soldier. Reprinted with permission of Picador/Pan Macmillan and The Permissions Company, LLC on behalf of Graywolf Press.

Library of Congress Cataloging-in-Publication Data

Names: Nguyen, Viet Thanh, 1971– author.

Title: To save and to destroy : writing as an other / Viet Thanh Nguyen.

Description: Cambridge, Massachusetts : The Belknap Press of Harvard University Press, 2025. | Series: The Charles Eliot Norton lectures, 2023–2024 | Includes bibliographical references and index.

Identifiers: LCCN 2024035448 (print) | LCCN 2024035449 (ebook) | ISBN 9780674298170 (cloth) | ISBN 9780674299764 (epub) | ISBN 9780674299771 (pdf)

Subjects: LCSH: Nguyen, Viet Thanh, 1971– | Other (Philosophy) in literature. | Minorities in literature. | Authorship—Philosophy. | Vietnamese Americans—California— San Jose—Biography. | Immigrants—California—San Jose—Biography. | Refugees— Vietnam—Buôn Mê Thuột—Biography. | LCGFT: Literary criticism. | Autobiographies. | Lectures.

Classification: LCC PN56.O69 N48 2025 (print) | LCC PN56.O69 (ebook) | DDC 813/.6—dc23/eng/20240828

LC record available at https://lccn.loc.gov/2024035448

LC ebook record available at https://lccn.loc.gov/2024035449

For my sister
Nguyễn Thị Thanh Hương

CONTENTS

TO SAVE AND TO DESTROY

PROLOGUE

To be self and other. To feel the power of stories and language. These two themes intertwine throughout literature. Narratives, for example, often persuade readers to identify with characters who are their others in some way, sometimes by not being exactly like the person reading, other times by belonging to categories of humanity seemingly far removed from the reader. Writers, too, grapple with otherness of various kinds in their texts, from the problems posed by enemies or strangers to the intimate dilemmas involving parents, children, neighbors, friends, and lovers. Language and the self can be others as well, and perhaps having an acute sense of this otherness in relation to one's own being and to language is necessary to become a writer.

Grappling with one's individual peculiarity or alienation differs, however, from having otherness imposed as a collective condition by external, even malevolent forces. A gulf also exists between those who would distance themselves from demonized others and those who are stigmatized in such a fashion. These Norton Lectures, carried out as both criticism and autobiography, are my attempt to think through what it means to write and read from the position of an other, which is for me the starting point of an ethical and political art.

Weaving between criticism and autobiography reflects my career as a scholar and my self-education as a writer, which began with being a refugee and the son of refugees fleeing from Việt Nam after the end of a war. Both academia and writing offered me havens from the travails of war and colonialism, as well as displacement and racism. But academia and writing were not only spaces of refuge. They were also sites of friction and struggle where I sought to break down the distinctions between the scholarly and the literary, as well as the artistic and the political, fumbling my way toward becoming a writer.

The belief that stories had the power to save me was one of my motivations: Save me by diverting me from boredom, despair, and loneliness, routine matters aggravated by the drama of refugee and postwar life and how it affected my parents. Rescue me by offering art and the imagination as alternative forms of reality that would allow me to analyze and depict this drama, and in so doing come to understand that war and the making of refugees are not incidental or marginal to the life of nation-states, but central.

This belief about stories offering salvation might be sentimental and self-serving for a storyteller, but if so, the sentimentality is alleviated by the possibility that stories could also save others by helping us confront, or at least articulate, the terror of abusive power and its manifestations in capitalism and colonialism, war and authoritarianism, patriarchy and its norms of sex and gender. Ultimately, stories could also brace us for the mystery of the end of our lives and those of our loved ones.

But if stories wield this power, they also have the capacity to destroy us or our others, our demons, our monsters. Stories and language have always been weaponized by individuals and societies, and anyone who has ever been marked as an other or outsider knows well the capacity of words, images, and narratives to caricature, marginalize, and eliminate, actions of symbolic violence that justify and foreshadow the physical violence conducted against those deemed less than human.

If my literary dreams began in the innocence of boyhood, with an uncomplicated love for enrapturing stories, my transformation into a writer was only possible through recognizing the complex power of stories and how they had shaped my own otherness, both the kind imposed on me by forces beyond my control and the otherness already hidden inside. Which form of otherness came first, I do not know, but part of the journey from innocence to experience meant understanding that the power of writing, once in my hands and those of many of the writers who inspired or provoked me, could be dangerous, even treacherous, since writing is itself an other to the writer.

In these lectures, I examine a selection of writers who have dealt with some of these matters and who have been meaningful to me, from the very famous and long departed to the still living whose literary fate remains to be determined. I begin with duality and speaking for others, challenges that I have also addressed in the book I was finishing when the invitation to deliver the Norton Lectures arrived: *A Man of Two Faces: A Memoir, a History, a Memorial.* Readers of that book will see that it provides the material for part of the first lecture and all of the second lecture, a transition that sets up *To Save and to Destroy* as a sequel where I continue working through some preoccupations around writing and otherness. Subsequent lectures address Israel's war on Gaza and Palestinians, the crossing of borders as both a migratory and literary act, the importance of being minor, and the possibility of finding joy in otherness.

The isolation that being other often produces and that writing requires can be lonely. But being lonely differs from being alone, which is a solace that writers and readers often seek. Their love of stories, typically experienced in private, paradoxically offers them the chance to create a literary community once they emerge from their solitude. As a result, the world is transformed for writers and readers, which is not to say that the world as a whole is remade. That kind of world-making requires readers to put their books down and take a different kind of action. But the gears of the world and the gears of the imagination interlock, and the scenarios fashioned in literary texts might yet impact the world that inspired them. So it is that the solidarity found among those like-minded others who create and read literature may find a corollary and a parallel with social and political movements that contest the imposed conditions of otherness, movements that depend on the storytelling ability to name injustice and to imagine a more just world.

Deploying this imagination to write through and about otherness might be daunting, given how otherness is most likely irresolvable, from the maze of our own psyches to the human need to create others against whom we define ourselves with violence of various kinds and degrees. My own otherness has often been perplexing and troublesome, as the task of writing has likewise been for me. And yet otherness and writing, along with the urgency of building literary and worldly communities, offer enough pleasure—a sometimes painful pleasure, to be sure—that I continue to heed their call, not least because one result of working at writing and writing through otherness is the possibility of creating beauty from horror and tragedy, a beauty found in both art and solidarity.

1.   ON THE DOUBLE,
OR INAUTHENTICITY

When I received the letter of invitation to deliver the Norton Lectures at Harvard, I was taken aback. I have been in academia more than three decades now, long enough to know that named chairs and lectureships mean *something*, even if I often do not know exactly what they mean, or who these names are. Was this Norton somehow related to W. W. Norton, the publisher? Or to the Norton anthologies of English literature? I diligently read those volumes as an undergraduate, for they presented a canon that I—good student, model minority, immigrant, refugee, outsider, other—felt he had to know. Clearly, however, I did not know the canon enough, for I needed to look up Charles Eliot Norton and the Norton Lectures. On seeing some of the names of those who have given these lectures, including e. e. cummings, who knew Norton and grew up in Cambridge, Massachusetts, I was dutifully and suitably impressed. I was raised in San José, California, and who knows the way to San José? Now knowing a little bit about this name of Norton, I confess that the rather large button of my vanity was pressed, and immediately after that, the even larger button of my insecurity. What was my name in comparison to these names?

Then I read some of the Norton Lectures, and after going through those of Italo Calvino, Jorge Luis Borges, Nadine Gordimer, and others, I could only conclude that Harvard had indeed erred. This invitation to speak was—is—a case of mistaken identity, me being mistaken for someone else who is also myself, another who also bears my name. This has happened to me before, more than once, since my first and last name are, together, rather common. I have a friend in Los Angeles, a television director also named Viet Nguyen, who has been mistaken for me a few times, from businesses where he offers his credit card to Hollywood functions. Then there was my senior year at the University of California, Berkeley, when I was in one of the English honors seminars. Very few Vietnamese Americans majored in English, but one of them was also named Viet Nguyen and he was enrolled in the other English honors seminar. My double was shorter than me and looked nothing like me, or perhaps looked exactly like me, depending on who was looking, like his professor. That professor was in charge of graduate admissions, and when I applied, mistook me for the other Viet Nguyen, whom he disliked. I was almost not admitted to Berkeley's doctoral program, and my life would have taken a perhaps radically different direction because of this other who wore my name.

Mistaken identity or not, I accepted this invitation to speak, mostly because of the challenge, which a good student never turns down, but honestly also partly because of the prestige, which a model minority is always seduced by, and even more honestly, because of the money. Crass, I know, to speak of money, especially so early in these lectures. But money is often an absent presence, speaking in the lower frequencies, at least for someone like me. I once knew how much I cost because after college, my father, frustrated by my careless way with money, gave me an itemized bill of all the expenses that my parents had paid for my existence. I wish I still had that invoice of myself. It was written in my father's hand, my father who can no longer calculate, can no longer write. I do not blame my father, for though he billed me, he never actually made me pay. His sacrifice, and my mother's, were gifts to me.

Born into rural poverty, a refugee twice, my father loved me, and when he remembers, loves me still. He would not charge me for my existence, but neither could he afford to ignore money. Nor could my mother. Also born into rural poverty, also a refugee twice, she told me once, when I was a teenager, how the twenty-pound sack of jasmine rice my parents sold in their grocery store in San José for twenty dollars netted her twenty-five cents in profit. Perhaps she exaggerated how little she made per sack, or maybe my memory is unreliable, especially given my inattentiveness with money and bills. But my mother intended to impart a lesson about labor and cost, pain and profit. About value and values. Each sack of rice, having absorbed some part of my mother's being, contributed to my care and education. My mother was and my father is a devout Catholic and a fervent capitalist, and their habits of sacrifice and struggle are my inheritance, even as I set out to acquire another kind of culture altogether, a different kind of faith, that has delivered me here to this lecture stage. If my parents wanted me to understand how their hard work and their belief in the cultures of capitalism and Catholicism had saved us from godless communism, I could not help but wonder what might have been destroyed by these cultures from which I gradually had become estranged.

This theme of salvation and destruction should be familiar enough to anyone who is or has been a devotee of a religion, including Catholicism, communism, or capitalism, the most fundamental of American creeds. Refugees also stand at this juncture between salvation and destruction. The spectacle of refugees, stranded on overcrowded boats or in squalid camps, raises an implicit question for those seeing them from a safe distance: will they live or die, be saved or destroyed? As a refugee myself, or having been a refugee, having spent time on the sea and in a camp, my origins and the potential crassness of refugees continues to influence, or taint, or haunt, or horrify me. As some refugees or former refugees have noted, determining when one ceases feeling like a refugee can be difficult, even if one is no longer a refugee in fact and by law, as in my case. Still, I locate my origins not only where I was born, Việt Nam, but also in the hollow of my memory, from which I emerged in a refugee camp in Pennsylvania. Without these origins, without my double who is and always will be a refugee, I would not be a writer, or at least not the kind of writer I am, inhabited by the reality of what a refugee is: a specimen of "bare life."

In the words of the philosopher Giorgio Agamben, "bare life" means being stripped of all the trappings of humanity, rendering one biologically alive but not human in a cultural, social, civilizational sense.[1] Bare life exists, Agamben argues, in both concentration camps and refugee camps. I would suggest that bare life is also found wherever the refugee is, on a boat or on foot, on the sea or in a jungle. Many of those refugees who survive their crossing or containment and become human again do their best to leave bare life behind, refusing, sometimes, even to call themselves refugees. They instead use a somewhat more palatable name for themselves: the immigrant. But perhaps the memory of that reduction to physical essence always clings to them, as stench, as shadow, as double. As an other that is also, at the same time, them.

Edward Said, one of my influences and role models, preferred the term "exile" over "refugee" to describe his own journey. In his elegant and melancholic essay "Reflections on Exile," he writes that "The word 'refugee' has become a political one, suggesting large herds of innocent and bewildered people requiring urgent international assistance, whereas 'exile' carries with it . . . a touch of solitude and spirituality."[2] The implication is rather clear. The exile has the capacity to be an exegetical figure, a writer or a scholar, while writers and scholars would rather become exiles than refugees. In Said's prose, a scent of romance, glamour, and artistic possibility lingers around exiles, even as they suffer—a perfume that cannot be detected around more malodorous refugees. The exile is human. The refugee is not.

As a graduate student in my early twenties, I once saw Said deliver a lecture in a crowded hotel ballroom at the Modern Language Association conference. The topic was opera, one of his passions. I understood all the words but very little of the meaning, having never seen an opera and never having heard one in its entirety. Said was a classical pianist, whereas my parents chose, as my musical instrument, an electronic organ with an illuminated keyboard so I could play "Ave Maria" and the rest of the church music they loved so much. I never did learn to play that organ. I also turned out an atheist. But I was aware that classical music and opera signified art and canon, taste and refinement, wealth and power, and I learned the names of the composers even if I did not know their music. From my vantage point at the back of the ballroom, I admired Said's erudition, his well-tailored suit, his august bearing, his enormous stature in the field. He seemed to belong completely to the Modern Language Association, and so I was struck many years later by the title of his memoir: *Out of Place.*

Said presumably knew he was, in some ways, an insider, someone laying the foundation for an entire field—postcolonialism—and someone whose surname carries at least as much weight as Norton's. I share Said's sentiments of being an insider, yet out of place, uneasily dwelling in the border zone of the other in the humanities and the arts, a liminal space often overlooked but occasionally illuminated by those celebrating or condemning us. Caught in the spotlight, I, or someone like me who bears my name, realizes he has consciously separated himself from the herd, presumably because he has a voice and can be heard, or so I think. The noises I utter are not those of beasts, although, once, when I gave a talk on war and memory, the professor who invited me to his seminar described my work as a cri de coeur.

I was impressed by his French. I am sure mine, in comparison, is terrible. Nevertheless, there will be a great deal of such cries from the heart in these six lectures. In the great duality between body and mind, people like me or somewhat like me who share in the vast and conflicted kinship of the other—refugees, so-called minorities of the racial, sexual, and other kinds, the colonized or the formerly colonized—are consigned to the space of the body, or perhaps our bodies occupy and preoccupy (some of) us. For a writer like me, working in fields where I should be defined by my voice, mind, and art, my stubborn body is my own double, my lingering, insistent connection to the world in which writers and critics refine texts.

I have mined my texts from my emotions and ideas, but those are embedded in my body. When I write or speak, I cannot forget my body, even if this invitation to give the Norton Lectures tempts me to speak purely in the voice of disembodied authority. If once I, or an earlier version of me, was reduced to bare life, that nakedness has by now been covered with the shroud of the humanities, the cloak of literature I have wrapped around myself. This culture of the humanities and the arts helped save me from my parents' Catholicism and capitalism, or so implied the charismatic professor who taught my survey of British literature. He lectured in suit and tie and proclaimed to hundreds of idealistic undergraduates that what we studied here, in English, mattered so much more than what those philistines in the business school did. I laughed, along with everyone else, reveling in our cultural superiority to the moneymakers. I do not remember if I thought about my parents, whom my professor might have seen as philistines, or maybe even less than philistines, since they had never even gone to college, much less business school. My parents knew how to make money, but not as masters.

Making money and talking about it is vulgar, while creating art and the scholarship that discusses it is refined, at least in the fields many artists and scholars find themselves in. And yet, part of what it means to be an other in the humanities and arts, at least in the West, which is a euphemism for the still-beating, still-glowing heart of colonial and global empire, is to be reminded on a fairly regular basis that one's otherness overlaps with one's value. That value fluctuates, based on the market conditions and fashionability of one's university, discipline, field, or art, as well as one's individual reputation and the estimation of the herd to which one belongs. Sometimes the other is devalued, at other times overvalued. If one happens to be that other, for whatever reason, one is marked by the X where two intersecting ways of being and belief meet. Pierre Bourdieu described these two ways of being and belief as invested in radically diametrical systems: economic value, on the one hand, and symbolic value, on the other.[3] Czeslaw Milosz, in his Norton Lectures, *The Witness of Poetry,* more poetically called this an opposition between the bohemian and the bourgeoisie or philistine.[4] They are each other's other, their worlds reversed. What the bourgeois or philistine esteems, the bohemian disdains, and vice versa. Those who toil in the bohemian field of cultural production, where symbolic value is created in the arts and humanities, might still be able to spin that symbolic value into economic value, or money, the other to art and poetry. This is how writers who may earn little money in the open market could still achieve a decent living in the university, the economic return on their symbolic value.

The symbolic and economic values of otherness, and how those values are created, extracted, and exploited, fascinate me. I am also compelled by the political and artistic possibilities of otherness and what it means to write as an other, one of the themes on which I will play through these six lectures. I want to think through what otherness means for writers who write about others, and for writers who may themselves be others. By *others,* I mean those who are outcast from or exploited by the powerful norm of their societies, or those who have moved voluntarily or have been moved forcefully from one place to another, or those who have been dominated in their own homes by outsiders whom they would consider to be others. By *others,* I also mean ourselves, for as Toni Morrison points out in her Norton Lectures, *The Origin of Others,* otherness emerges from within the mysterious and unknown, or at best partly known, territory inside us all, a nexus of fears and desires we project onto those whom we label strangers, foreigners, enemies, invaders, threats.[5]

The literature of those who could be called others in some way has been my preoccupation for many years. Writing and otherness is also an autobiographical theme, as I have long felt myself to be an other in some manner, both as an other to others but also, as I have come to realize, as an other to myself. This was one of my more painful realizations as I became a writer and began to vivisect myself rather than only dissecting texts. For me, to write about others is also to write from the position of an other. Rather than pretend that my autobiography and my body have nothing to do with my critical theme, I acknowledge my refugee roots. This is a paradox, as refugees are, by definition, uprooted. No more paradoxical, however, than to think of refugees as alive but not human, which is also how others are often perceived by those who do not see themselves as other.

Money, too, is alive but not human. Money possesses an existence of its own, a life deemed by many to be much more valuable than the lives of others. Otherness can be traded for money, or otherness can be exploited for it, from the enterprises of capitalism and colonialism to the work of art and culture. These intersections of otherness and value are serious and oftentimes tragic matters, for others and otherness are created through the brutal encounters of war, enslavement, and genocide, as well as the hierarchies of class, capital, and labor, and the slow violence of patriarchy and its norms of sex and gender. But these tragic matters, which seem to demand our reverence or our refutation, can also be absurd. Isn't that what we mean when, confronted by some bizarre situation, we say, "You've got to be joking!" The joke, however, is often on us, the other, including the other in the humanities and the arts. In the West, humanities and the arts, besides being crucial endeavors in exploring and celebrating the human, also function at least partially to obscure the viciousness of the conquests and exploitation that have made the West the West and the other the other.

Rithy Panh, the greatest commemorator of the Cambodian genocide, points out this obfuscation in his book *The Elimination,* where he argues that while the genocide is the responsibility of the Khmer people, it is also the culmination of Western civilization, a tragedy overseen by an elite of Khmer students who studied Western philosophy in Paris. This tragedy and absurdity occasions the following joke in *Afterparties,* the short story collection by Anthony Veasna So that focuses on Cambodian refugees and their descendants in California. In one story, a father who is a Khmer survivor of the horror that killed about 1.7 million people says that the television reality show "*Survivor* was actually the most Khmer thing possible, and he would definitely win it, because the genocide was the best training he could've got."[6] This laugh of the other in the face of devastation is a critical artistic and political strategy, although So's irreverence toward something as sacred as the genocide might only be possible for a descendant one generation removed.

In another of So's stories, his gay narrator describes himself as a "girly wimp" and a "precocious freak who came out before puberty." Responding to his open gayness, his mother says, "It's hard enough for people like us." She means Khmer refugees from Cambodia, including herself and her husband, whom the narrator calls "immigrant parents." Coming out to these immigrant parents is, the narrator says, "All very cliché, in that gay sob story kind of way, but I can't explain it any better than that."[7] The sob story—gay, refugee, immigrant, Asian, or otherwise—is perhaps the dominant kind of story the other is expected to tell and to sell, especially to readers who seek insight into the condition of the other who is supposedly defined by trauma. Not just trauma in general but one and only one specific trauma, the trauma which belongs to this other and to which this other is bound, the trauma both giving the other value and also devaluing the other.

The poet Bao Phi addresses this lure to speak of trauma, and the ensuing trap of trauma, in his book *Sông I Sing*. In one poem, he writes about Vietnamese refugees who came to the United States and resettled in Louisiana, where decades later Hurricane Katrina displaced them once more. The poet connects the experiences of war refugees and climate refugees, but he encounters resistance from some in his audience:

> It's like this country only allows us one grief at a time.
> Your people, you had that war thing. That's all you get.
> Shut. The fuck. Up.[8]

Bao Phi is ventriloquizing the skeptics in his audience, amplifying their sotto voce dismissal of others who dare to claim more than their allotted grief. I think of Caliban, the native from Shakespeare's *The Tempest,* and his most famous line, addressed to his alien master, the invader and colonizer of his island, his own other, Prospero: "You taught me language, and my profit on't / Is, I know how to curse."[9] Caliban presumably spoke another language before Prospero's arrival, but all Prospero heard was gibberish or gobbledygook—not a language at all. The incomprehensibility is so dangerous that the master would rather teach the native his own language so that if the native cursed him, he could understand.

The curse and the laugh of the other help writers to avoid the first of three major temptations in writing about others. The first temptation is to idealize or sentimentalize, to turn the other into angel or victim, to disguise the faults of the other or exaggerate the other's pain. Salman Rushdie dispels this temptation in his essay "Is Nothing Sacred?" After the fatwa directed against him and *The Satanic Verses,* he was referring to Mohammed, to his novel, to himself. His answer was no, nothing is sacred, not even literature, which might disturb writers who treat literature as holy. So it is with one's own otherness. Given how others are erased, distorted, and dehumanized in literature not written by them, the temptation to revere one's otherness is understandable. It is nevertheless a weakness, perhaps the most common vulnerability in the literature written by others, who may be tempted to treat the trauma of the other as sacred, to treat the other as holy.

In contrast, canonical literature, the literature of high value, is replete with white men depicting white men doing terrible deeds, as in Joseph Conrad's *Heart of Darkness,* which helped to inspire Francis Ford Coppola's *Apocalypse Now.* The freedom to show people like oneself being monstrous is a freedom that we others might be tempted to reject, not realizing that in so doing, we deny ourselves the full power of art, which comes from grappling with the otherness inside of ourselves, this otherness we may wish to deny because of the ways we have been demonized.

I first fully encountered my own otherness when I saw *Apocalypse Now* at the age of eleven or twelve, experiencing the shock of misrecognition so commonplace to those who discover how we perceive ourselves is not how others see us. Being unsettled through misrecognition is a classic moment in the constitution of the other, recounted by many, including Chinua Achebe in the lectures he gave at Harvard, published as *Home and Exile*. Required to read the acclaimed novel *Mister Johnson* by Joyce Cary, a white man writing about Africa, Achebe and his high school classmates rebelled against their white teacher. "What his book *Mister Johnson* did for me," Achebe remembers, "was to call into question my childhood assumption of the innocence of stories."[10] What Achebe found in *Mister Johnson* was, among other things, how "The enslavement and expatriation of Africans was a blessing; and not even a blessing in disguise, but a blessing that is clearly recognizable! A blessing that delivered the poor wretches from a worse fate in their homeland!"[11]

My family were among the wretched, if from a different homeland. We had been delivered from the worse fate of communism to the promised land of the American Dream, or so many Americans understood this history. This story of American salvation also framed me when I experienced my shock of misrecognition. The setting: our living room in San José where I read the Sunday edition of the *San Jose Mercury News* from cover to cover, including the book review, one of my portals into the world of literary taste. I had the house to myself every weekend because my parents worked at their grocery store, leaving me in solitude and spirituality, but not of the religious kind. My secular spirituality was found first in books and then movies, watched on a VCR. Communing with stories saved me from the loneliness of being a refugee child of refugee parents. But if stories were powerful enough to save me, *Apocalypse Now* was my first encounter with a story powerful enough to destroy me.

This loss of my childhood illusions and innocence about stories, this scene of my otherness, takes place in the middle of *Apocalypse Now,* when American sailors on a gunboat come across a sampan of Vietnamese civilians. The movie is told from the perspective of Captain Willard, the Marlowe figure who journeys into the heart of darkness of white men, including himself. As a boy, I was already a veteran of watching American propaganda, which is to say war movies and westerns. I viewed this movie through the eyes of the Americans, of whom I considered myself one, until the moment the sailors massacred the Vietnamese civilians, who were not yet refugees but who fit Said's description of refugees as an "innocent" and "bewildered" herd. When Willard fired a bullet into a Vietnamese woman's chest, I was split in two. Was I the American doing the killing, or the Vietnamese being killed?

The movie's depiction of actually existing physical violence against the Vietnamese, which some interpret as an antiwar statement, also constitutes an act of renewed symbolic violence against the Vietnamese. Said described the interlocking nature of physical and symbolic violence against Orientals in his book *Orientalism,* just as Morrison articulated these same processes against Africans and African Americans in *The Origin of Others* and throughout her body of work. Each mode of violence—physical and symbolic—justified and perpetuated the other, each one capable of saving or destroying the other. In the realm of symbolic violence, the true violation was not primarily the depiction of killing others but the silencing of others and rendering them purely as victims, innocent and bewildered. Having grown up in a refugee herd, I felt that bewilderment was only part of our Vietnamese sentiments. What about rage, sadness, melancholy, bitterness, resentment, affection, and love? As for our innocence, what about the domestic abuse, gang violence, adultery, alcoholism, or economic predation inflicted by some of us upon each other and the government, not to mention the assassinations?

If we others were shown doing such terrible things by those more powerful than us, it was not because we were complex antiheroes suffering from the tragedy of our misguided deeds, but because we were inscrutable villains who derived sadistic pleasure from our crimes. In contrast, how was it possible for white men to depict white men committing atrocities while convincing me and millions of others to read and watch them doing so repeatedly, up until the present? The answer is that the awesome physical violence depicted on screen, which also happened in real life, was matched by the sublime symbolic violence of the depiction itself, whether found in movies or books or in the entire industry of representation. No surprise that those subjected to symbolic violence might react by engaging in a defensive reflex of the herd— demanding that only sob stories be told about them by others and by themselves to enhance their innocence, vulnerability, and victimhood, camouflaging themselves in the guise of humanity, hoping for a mercy that may or may not come, a mercy which depends on the guns, cameras, and pens of the hunters and the masters.

Along with this temptation of idealization and purification as a mode of symbolic self-defense, the writer as other has a second temptation: to separate oneself from the herd, to become less of a target by paradoxically becoming more visible, more individual, and perhaps, in that way, more human. Separating from the herd is to internalize in oneself the already existing strategy of master and colonizer to divide others and conquer them, subjugating the many and rewarding the few. This internalization of the master's logic is seen in Aimé Césaire's *A Tempest,* his rewriting of *The Tempest* from Caliban's perspective. Caliban becomes Prospero's match, a figure of decolonizing violence that repudiates Shakespeare's rendering of him. I laughed a great deal at the play's angry satire when I saw it staged at the Berkeley Repertory Theatre as a student, but the older white couple next to me didn't laugh at all. Perhaps Césaire's play puzzled them precisely because it could incite the laugh of the other through reversing Shakespeare's play, with the power and limitations that turning the tables implies.

In Césaire's version, facing Prospero before their final battle, Caliban at last says his truth blunt and simple: "I hate you." Is "I hate you" the right response to Prospero's hatred of Caliban, which he masks with paternal benevolence? Hatred may be an effective political emotion, but it is also spiritually corrosive, a human response entwined with inhumanity, with the victim potentially becoming the victimizer, an other aspiring to mastery. We all exist at this juncture of humanity and inhumanity, but one definition of others is that they are relegated to only one or the other side of this contradiction, human or inhuman, but not both. The aesthetic and political response of others must be to claim both sides of the double, as well as everything in between, which is what the masters have always done to great effect. In other words, *Heart of Darkness* and *Apocalypse Now,* inasmuch as they desecrate the natives, are still important works of art for some, including me.

I have tried to absorb their troubling power in my novels *The Sympathizer* and *The Committed,* whose protagonist is his own double, a man of two faces and two minds. Being of two minds, he is too smart for his own good. Spy, womanizer, alcoholic, liar, traitor, murderer, but still, hopefully, rather likable. A Caliban, of sorts, or at least Césaire's Caliban. A victim, but also more than that. As an innocent, he also wants to do harm. Both human and inhuman, he is the tragic and antiheroic protagonist of his own drama. But he is not just a figure for the native, savage, enslaved, or colonized. Knowing language and knowing how to curse, he might also be a writer. He is certainly irritable enough, and irritating enough, to be a writer. If he—Césaire's Caliban, but also my spy—is such a creature, then Caliban's curse is not that he can curse. His curse is to be alone.

To separate oneself from the herd is also, in the West, to heed the call of the bohemian, the artist who is, in Milosz's words, an alien from his own society. I think about the poet Arthur Rimbaud's line, "*Je est un autre,*" "I is another."[12] Rimbaud was certainly an other to bourgeois society, and his case gestures at how otherness is experienced individually, including by artists who voluntarily take on their own otherness, or are seized by it. One difference between Rimbaud and Caliban, however, is that Caliban's otherness is also imposed on him by his master. Inasmuch as Caliban is an allegorical figure for the native in both Shakespeare and Césaire's versions, his otherness is collective as well as individual.

Perhaps Caliban could say instead, "We is an other." In both *The Tempest* and *A Tempest,* however, collective possibility is foreclosed to Caliban. His mother is dead, Ariel has sided with Prospero, the white men with whom he allies himself are fools. Césaire, adopting Shakespeare's setting, only has a deserted island to give to Caliban, instead of an island populated with other natives with whom Caliban could cultivate solidarity. "We is an other" expresses a solidarity necessary to combat, both politically and aesthetically, the conditions of otherness. But that solidarity, that we-ness, could also be the condition furthering the writer's alienation as an other. While these communities of our otherness can assuage solitude and be the source for stories, they also could be the limit, particularly if writers struggle under what has been called the "burden of representation." Mirror image to the white man's burden, this burden of representation demands that writers tell idealized, sanitized, or stereotyped stories about their communities, kneeling before the sacred as they attempt to carry out salvation through stories.

This obligation to a sacred community, whether that be family, culture, religion, or nation, is important but also constitutes the third temptation of otherness, which is to see the other as an identity. As an identity, however defined, the other is something or someone authentic and hence knowable and definable. Seeing the other in this fashion, one might be tempted to think one can know, master, or own the representation of this authentic other, without understanding that the real power of otherness lies in its inherent inauthenticity. Jacques Derrida describes this in *Monolingualism of the Other,* where the philosopher provides glimpses of his own autobiographical otherness as an Algerian-born French Jew, out of place amid Algerians and their French colonizers. After the Algerian revolution against France in the 1950s and 1960s, Derrida was eventually forced to move to France. But he refuses to write a full-blown memoir, to narrate his otherness in a cohesive manner and hence to fix himself into the identity of an other. His interest is focused instead on how otherness is always elusive, even to the other. Is there anything more contradictory than to write a memoir of being an other, when otherness, including our own, is something that we ultimately cannot grasp?

Derrida suggests an autobiographical link between his youthful experiences in Algeria and his eventual philosophical concerns with the elusiveness of meaning in language. For Derrida, it is (im)possible to master language, an idea I had not considered as I began to harbor dreams of being a writer. By college, I was intent on mastering English language and literature in order to demonstrate through my writing that I—and we, as Asian Americans, as others—belonged in a country, the United States, that saw us as foreigners, our alienness defined partly by our "weird English."[13] But what if writing in itself is an other to the writer? To be or to become a writer is in some ways to feel as if one has been called, as if writing has chosen the writer as much as vice versa. Writing as an other is a lure, a compulsion, a temptation to and an illusion of mastery. But masters are not always masterful. They are sometimes undermined, by others or by themselves. As for the Asian American desire to belong to this country, the other's desire to be counted among the masters, owners, and settlers is not without complication.

The deluded master appears in Herman Melville's *Moby-Dick*, which I studied for my doctoral qualifying examination in American literature, and which also appears in *Afterparties*. In one of the stories, a high school teacher, Cambodian American and gay, contemplates teaching *Moby-Dick* to his students. No surprise that a Cambodian American high school teacher and a Vietnamese American doctoral student in English would both meditate on this master text of the American canon. For the school teacher, who is his high school's "Endowed Teaching Fellow for Diversity,"[14] the white whale symbolized a "failed promise of closure,"[15] while the novel itself "didn't care for resolutions."[16] My take on *Moby-Dick* differed when I was a Predoctoral Minority Fellow at Berkeley. *Moby-Dick* was one of many texts I read in my field of nineteenth-century American literature, but a text to which my professor devoted half of my exam. He focused on only one scene, where Ahab nails a doubloon of the "purest, virgin gold" to the mast of his ship, a reward for the man who would first spy the white whale.[17] I no longer remember what I said about the doubloon, but I am certain I nailed my answers, qualifying to master American literature, or, perhaps, to doctor it.

My desire for mastery was rooted in being an other, or feeling myself to be one. If I wanted the prestige and power of mastery, even if only the mastery of literature, I also wanted what the men of the *Pequod* wanted, what my fellow graduate students yearned for: the gold doubloon, or rather, the tenure track professorship. Not that we ever said this so crudely, unless we had lost hope about obtaining this job that promised intellectual satisfaction, and, if we dared to say it out loud, economic fulfillment. If I had not yet discerned that I could never master language any more than I could master literature, I also had no idea that the tenure track professorship, the prize that signaled an ascent to mastery in academia, might also be the entryway into a university that is, as a corporation, at least as capitalistic and hierarchical as a whaling ship.

Ahab's pursuit of the white whale is another enactment of the master being destroyed by his other, although it is not only the white whale who embodies and symbolizes that irresolvable otherness already inside of Ahab, the white male. So does the gold doubloon, which hailed my parents and, admittedly, me, making promises of fulfillment and even ecstasy it could not keep, like writing itself. While the doubloon was nailed to the mast, it also inhabited us, occupied us. Whether I was refugee, exile, or immigrant, I could see the glint of that gold doubloon, shining like the city on a hill across the Pacific, glowing like the green light on the faraway dock beckoning to Jay Gatsby, who was also someone aspiring to mastery, also a storyteller undercut by his own otherness in the eyes of others and himself.

If the doubloon symbolized one kind of otherness embodied in capitalism, then writing was antagonist and antidote. And yet writing remained an other to myself and to my parents, to whom I did not dare explain my writerly ambitions. I was supposed to become a doctor like my older brother, graduate of Harvard. Instead I became a doctor of English. Forget that the doctor of philosophy is the original doctor. Now the PhD is the phony doctor, at least in the eyes of many refugees and immigrants. But being a writer was even worse, for what use was writing?

Perhaps I instinctively understood that uselessness was precisely what was useful about writing in a world that valued the doubloon. In this world, my parents relied on capitalism to save their lives and mine, which also meant saving our souls. But if the soul elevates the human above the bare life of the refugee to which we had once been reduced, I somehow knew writing would save my life and soul. Either turn, however, to capitalism or writing would be an imperfect means of salvation, given capitalism and literature's power to annihilate as much as to save.

One last example of the writer as other and as double, wavering between authenticity and inauthenticity, salvation and destruction. In Percival Everett's novel *Erasure,* the novelist Thelonious Ellison is fed up with the Blackness projected onto him and his work. Deciding to feed white ideas of Blackness back to white readers, he writes a novel of Black otherness so extreme he assumes readers will say: You've got to be joking! He submits the novel pseudonymously under the title *My Pafology.* A producer immediately wants to buy the rights for three million dollars (and *Erasure* would eventually be turned into the movie *American Fiction*). Sensing that people are not getting the joke, Thelonious Ellison amplifies his parody by changing the novel's title to one word: *Fuck.*

"Why not *Hell* or *Damn?*" his agent says.

His otherwise enthusiastic editor says, "It might hurt sales."

The novelist insists. Of course, the joke is on him, when the novel becomes more successful than anything written under his own name. Meanwhile, he has agreed to serve on a literary prize jury. Unexpectedly, or expectedly, the novel is shortlisted for the prize and Thelonious Ellison has to confront his own monstrous pseudonym and double, Stagg R. Leigh, when Leigh wins the book award. The doubloon is bestowed on the buffoon.

No joke, but definitely a curse.

Into this tragicomic conundrum, the writers who are others must nevertheless fall and rise, fall and fail, again and again, as they confront, avoid, exploit, or elevate their own otherness, both the difference projected onto them and the alterity already entwined inside. This otherness and its history demands grief, but the challenge of the writer as an other is to expand that grief, to make it ever more capacious, rather than reduce it to a singular sorrow. Capacious grief acknowledges that the trauma of the other is neither singular nor unique, that there are other others out there with whom we can share the burden. Perhaps only by expanding our grief might we be able to leave our trauma behind. And in sharing our burden—of writing, of representation, of otherness—we might transform that burden into a gift.

2. ON SPEAKING FOR AN OTHER

My mother gave me a gift whose significance has grown with me over time—her love. This gift, expressed through her unwavering belief in me, who had done nothing to deserve it, played no small part in my becoming a writer. Thanks to my mother, I have been able to confront the challenge of writing with the same kind of stubbornness that she brought to her endeavors. But while Má was to me a hero who lived an epic life and survived an epic journey, I have to acknowledge that in the end she was undone, like so many other heroes, by the only person who could defeat her: herself. This was a purely private affair for her and her family, until I chose to write about her and speak on her behalf in a memoir that she did not ask for.

Perhaps it is not true, then, that she was undone only by herself. Perhaps I, too, in attempting to share my sorrow, to engage in capacious grief, have also undone her. Me and myself, writer and traitor.

This journey toward betrayal began in 2009 when I published a short story called "War Years," which is a somewhat autobiographical account of a boy growing up in San José, California, in the 1970s and 1980s, with parents who own a Vietnamese grocery store, which my parents called the SàiGòn Mới. I titled the story "War Years" because I could not separate that era of the grocery store from the shadow of the American war in Việt Nam. In the story, I described my mother as she appeared to me in my childhood: "Whenever she spoke in English, her voice took on a higher pitch, as if instead of coming from inside her, the language was outside, squeezing her by the throat."[1] In retrospect, I wonder if it was, in fact, my language in my hands around Má's neck, making her speak? And if I was finding my voice as a writer, how much of it was due to speaking for others, beginning first of all with my mother?

Unbeknownst to Má, she was raising one of the most frightening creatures you can ever find in your house: a writer. I wrote and drew my first book when I was in the third grade, around 1980, not long after she and my father opened the SàiGòn Mới, perhaps the second Vietnamese grocery store in San José. My father and mother worked twelve to fourteen hours, seven days a week, almost every day of the year. As a result, I was good at being alone, spending most of my time with books and stories rather than with people. My father thought that reading too much in dim light had led to me wearing glasses by the second grade, but if so, that reading had another effect: it fired my imagination, where I could see perfectly. So, when my third-grade teacher told us to write and draw our own books, I was ready. The title of my work: *Lester the Cat*.

> Lester was an urban cat, stricken with ennui.
> Bored of city life, he fled to the countryside.
> There, in a hay-strewn barn, he found love with a country cat.

The story was playful, although I did not realize at the time that Lester, yearning to escape, might stand in for me. Surprisingly, the San José Public Library gave *Lester the Cat* a book award, giving me my first taste of literary fame and setting me on the path to over thirty years of misery in trying to become a writer. My school librarian, a kindly, white-haired woman, took me to the award ceremony. There was a hotel across the street from the library, and she treated me to a hamburger at the hotel restaurant, which in my eight-year-old mind was the fanciest place I had ever been. My family were refugees, and we only ever ate out at a phở restaurant, after Vietnamese language mass on Sundays. This was long before phở was fashionable, when the only people present were Vietnamese and the only language spoken was Vietnamese. We all ate phở the ambidextrous Vietnamese way, chopsticks in one hand, spoon in the other, surrounded by the hubbub of Vietnamese voices.

The phở restaurant was part of an international chain spread across the Vietnamese refugee diaspora. Years later I heard rumors that the chain was funneling profits to the exiled remnants of the South Vietnamese army, intent on taking back Việt Nam from the victorious communists. San José was home to one of the largest populations of Vietnamese refugees in the world, and during our community celebrations like Tết, Vietnamese veterans in camouflage uniforms guarded the gates. We sang the South Vietnamese national anthem, and in the exhibition hall of the Tết festival, I saw photos of South Vietnamese guerrillas, somewhere in a jungle, training to invade Việt Nam.

My parents were anticommunist too, but they were more intent on saving our lives than fighting wars. Saving our lives meant working themselves to exhaustion at the SàiGòn Mới in pursuit of their American Dream, which is why neither of my parents could take me to the library for my award, and which is why, perhaps, Lester had neither a father nor a mother.

I felt more at home in this library, a massive white cube named after Martin Luther King, Jr., than I did in our house with its iron bars on all the windows, next to the entrance ramp to Interstate 280. When I was sixteen, a young white man followed my parents home from the SàiGòn Mới, broke into our house, and aimed his gun in all our faces, a scene I describe in "War Years." When the gunman told us to get on our knees, I, the coward, silently obeyed, as did my father. Ba, like me, was very good at self-preservation, although Ba, unlike me, had been tested by history and forced to make life-and-death decisions before, like the time he and my mother chose to become refugees in 1954, fleeing from the north of Việt Nam to the south, and the second time in 1975, when they chose to flee Việt Nam to come to the United States. These decisions, they told me often, saved us.

On this summer evening in 1987, my mother surprised all of us by dashing past the gunman and running screaming into the street. When the gunman turned to follow Má, Ba slammed the door shut on him, locking him outside.

With Má.

I saw her through the living room window but I couldn't hear her voice as she ran past all the cars heading for the freeway, running to save our lives.

My bedroom window had a view of this freeway entrance ramp, and that night, as I watched a stream of cars ascend the ramp, I wondered where they were going, and longed to go with them. The library offered me a way out. Inside the library was a world without borders for a refugee boy who, unlike his parents, had not chosen to cross borders. Books could deliver me across time and space, away from the house with its barred windows, away from the SàiGòn Mới, where Ba Má had been shot in their store on Christmas Eve.

I was nine. My brother and I were home alone. I was watching cartoons. Seven years older, my brother took the phone call. When he told me, I kept watching cartoons. What's the matter with you? my brother said. He was crying. I was not. I kept watching cartoons. My father and mother returned to work at the SàiGòn Mới within a day or two. They had to live, and to live they had to work, and they only had flesh wounds. We never spoke of that incident again.

So, when my parents could not make it to my award ceremony the next year, who was I to say anything? They were working to save our lives, and not just ours, but all the relatives back in a starving Việt Nam, including my parents' parents and my sister. Our hometown, Ban Mê Thuột, was the first one captured in the final invasion by the north in 1975. Ba was in Sài Gòn. Má, by herself, decided to flee with my brother and me and leave behind our sister, at age sixteen, to safeguard by herself the family property, which the victorious communists confiscated anyway. I had no memory of my grandparents or this sister, whom I last saw when I was four. Growing up in our San José house of barred windows, I was aware of absent presences, of ghosts, of missing persons, of the faces of my grandparents in black-and-white pictures, gazing at me in silence. All these others died before I could return to Việt Nam and hear their voices.

Part of me longed to hear the voices of Vietnamese people, even as another part of me didn't want to hear. I had come to the United States at age four fluent in Vietnamese, and all these decades later, my Vietnamese is still so fluent that when I go to Việt Nam, people compliment me on how good my Vietnamese is—for a Korean. My monolingualism, my linguistic infantilism, is one of the things that makes me an American. My resistance to Vietnamese came about because I grew up as an American, and my poor parents, aware they were raising an American alien in their household, sent me to Vietnamese Catholic Sunday school, which was the quickest way to guarantee that I would never learn or speak Vietnamese.

And yet I yearned to hear the voices of Vietnamese people because, as an American, I understood how Americans saw and heard, or didn't hear, Vietnamese people, who were among the many others in the American imagination. I was an American, which meant that America's others were also mine, born from what the poet William Carlos Williams called the "orgy of blood" that is American history.[2] But I also became aware of myself as an other through watching almost all of Hollywood's Vietnam War movies, an exercise I recommend to no one, especially if you are Vietnamese. When Americans said Việt Nam, they really meant the Vietnam War, but whether they meant the country or the war, "Vietnam" for Americans was an American drama, an American civil war, a conflict in the American soul in which we were the extras. This was our country and this was our war, and yet our only place in American movies was to be killed, raped, threatened, or rescued. All we could do was scream, cry, beg, threaten, or curse, and if we could say anything at all, it was either "Me love you long time" or "thank you" for being rescued. Of course, we were never so rude as to mention, at least in English, that we wouldn't have needed to be rescued by Americans if we hadn't been invaded by them in the first place.

The situation in the library was not much better. The books about Việt Nam were mostly about the war, and therefore mostly about Americans. There was a well-intentioned children's book about a Vietnamese refugee, but I didn't recognize myself in its world of rice paddies, water buffalo, and half-naked peasant boys. I finally found the novel *Blue Dragon White Tiger* by Trần Văn Dĩnh, a diplomat writing about the war from a South Vietnamese point of view and perhaps the first Vietnamese writer to write fiction in English. He said, "I am a Vietnamese by birth, an American by choice,"[3] and an echo of it must have stuck in my head, for decades later I would write, "I was born in Việt Nam, but made in America."[4] His novel put another thought in my head: we could write about our own experiences, in English, which was an other tongue that took the place of my mother tongue.

Outside of this book, however, almost all of my reading in this second home of the library was not about me or anyone who looked like me. Almost everything I read was by and about white people, and through those books, and through TV and the movies, also almost all about white people, I became an anthropologist of white people, knowing them far, far better than they knew me or those like me. One of the things I knew that white people expected of people like us—Vietnamese, refugees, others—was that we be grateful for our rescue by the United States. Perhaps I thought the best way to say "thank you" in English was to master English. As an adolescent in provincial San José, I became an Anglophile, in love with Dickens and Austen, Byron and Shelley, *Vanity Fair* and *Tom Brown's Schooldays*.

I am happy to report that after spending thirty years as a graduate student and a professor in English departments, I have been cured of my Anglophilia. But I did not know any better at seventeen and became an English major in college, then continued for a PhD in English. Reading, in English, was the one thing I was good at. Even though Berkeley's English department disciplined me into the canon by having me read the whole of English literature, I hung onto this stubborn desire to hear Vietnamese voices and write Vietnamese stories. At the same time, I also struggled to find my voice. In my English graduate seminars and later as a professor in English department faculty meetings, I barely said a word, feeling inauthentic, an imposter, a trespasser, an other. When I did speak, I wondered if I was speaking for myself, or if I was speaking for an other?

At home, with my parents, I also barely said a word. I had told my parents I was going to become a doctor. Really, they said? An English doctor, I said. Their faces fell. How could I explain to my parents that I loved reading Jane Austen and the Romantics? That I had discovered Asian American literature, which had saved me because it showed me that a writer could look like me, and that I could look like a writer? How could I say that as a writer, while I was still an other to many, even to myself, I could also find a voice in literature to assert my self?

This was impossible to explain because the language my parents and I shared, Vietnamese, was a stunted one because of me. And yet, as stunted as that language was, the language that I had mastered—English— gave me access to much of the world because its speakers had mastered that world, through invasion, enslavement, colonialism, warfare, and capitalism.

Still, I dedicated myself to this complicated tongue, an act inseparable from becoming an Asian American, a person of color, and someone just beginning to understand that he had been colonized and needed to decolonize himself. I read the literatures of peoples of color and anticolonial struggle, and in 1991 Maxine Hong Kingston admitted me to her nonfiction writing seminar of fourteen students. She was the author of *The Woman Warrior,* already a feminist and American literary classic reputed to be the most widely taught book on college campuses at the time. I was nineteen years old, a self-styled political activist. Every day,

I would sit down in seminar, a few feet from Kingston, and every day, I would fall asleep. At the end of the semester, she wrote me a letter in which she advised me to seek counseling. I never did. Instead, I became a writer.

Perhaps Kingston knew I was troubled because I wrote about my mother in her seminar. Then I put those essays about Má into a milk crate and put the milk crate into my bedroom closet. Thirty years passed before I could muster the will to return to those words and confront my awkward self and what it was that I refused to remember. During those three decades of misery, I did find my voice and become a writer. My first novel, *The Sympathizer,* was unexpectedly successful despite having been rejected by thirteen out of fourteen publishers. As one editor put it in his rejection, he "just had too much trouble crawling all the way inside the voice."[5] I understood why, especially given how I had spent a lifetime, ever since my earliest days in the San José Public Library, crawling all the way inside the voices of so many white writers.

When those white writers were writing, did they imagine they would be speaking to a young Vietnamese refugee boy? Probably not. Was I nevertheless spoken to, even though they were other to me? Yes. Because their voices were beautiful, and because I knew that if I wanted to survive in this country, I had to keep quiet and listen to these other voices, these masterful voices. One lesson I learned intuitively was that all those white writers I read and admired didn't need, and shouldn't need, to worry about whether a young Vietnamese refugee boy was ever going to read them. It was not their obligation. Therefore, the lesson I had to learn consciously was that I—a writer who also happens to be a Vietnamese refugee writer and an Asian American writer—didn't need to and shouldn't need to worry about whether non-Vietnamese people would read me. My obligation was *not* to care about whether anyone— white, Black, or otherwise—could crawl into my voice. My obligation was to speak as if everyone could already understand what I said.

That is an assumption a person of the so-called majority makes all the time, an assumption born from the privilege of being the beneficiary of imperialism, colonialism, racism, and patriarchy. A person of a so-called minority may find it hard to make this assumption. At least, it was difficult for me. To find my voice, I stopped thinking of myself only as a minority, even though I still sometimes find myself to be the only Asian in a room of many people. But I am not a minority if I think of myself as being part of a world, a globe, where white people are the minority. I am also not a minority if, when I am writing, I write first of all to myself, because I contain multitudes. And I am not a minority if I write to Vietnamese people. Everyone else can listen in.

In *The Sympathizer,* I constructed a narrative in which the protagonist, a spy of French and Vietnamese ancestry, is confessing to his Vietnamese military interrogator. If a Vietnamese person speaks to another Vietnamese person, there is no translation. If I were to write, in the voice of our narrator, "I would like a bowl of phở comma a delicious beef noodle soup comma"—then a sensitive reader would know that I am not talking to Vietnamese people. I would be translating for non-Vietnamese readers. People of the so-called majority, used to never translating themselves, used to always being translated to, might not notice this translation, this catering, this invitation to crawl inside the voice of the writer who has domesticated his otherness by turning himself into a translator. But imagine how you would feel if F. Scott Fitzgerald, in an early draft of *The Great Gatsby,* wrote, "Daisy made me a sandwich comma two slices of bread between which there is something delicious comma."

Fitzgerald would not translate because he assumes his audience knows what a sandwich is, or should know. And that is the right stance to take. So, so-called minority writers: do not translate. And readers of so-called minority literature: do not expect or demand translation. Translation, at least within a book written by a so-called minority, is more often than not a deformation of a voice, the sign of the so-called minority accepting their subjugated status. For me, refusing to translate was crucial to denying subjugation and otherness, a challenge inextricable from finding and claiming my voice. Refusing to translate was also my way of refusing to be a representative of Vietnamese people. Too often, so-called minority writers are expected to be the translators and representatives of their people, even when they are just writing fiction or poetry, a burden not usually placed on so-called majority writers. It was not a surprise, then, that a major book review of *The Sympathizer* called me "a voice for the voiceless." I thought, have you ever eaten at a Vietnamese restaurant? Visited a Vietnamese home? Hung out with Vietnamese people? We're really, really loud.

As Arundhati Roy puts it, "There's really no such thing as the 'voiceless.' There are only the deliberately silenced, or the preferably unheard."[6]

What does it mean, then, for someone to find their voice, when they are told that their voice is heard so much more clearly against the voicelessness of those others who are just like them? Those who want to hear "a voice for the voiceless" may actually be just as invested in *not* hearing the cacophony and the chorus of those they assume to be voiceless, those whom they have silenced, those whom they refuse to hear. It's easier to listen just to the one voice.

This is one reason why I reject the notion of the writer as only being a solitary artist whose task it is to find her or his or their voice. Much of the writer's work is solitary, of course, and during my thirty years of misery, I spent thousands of hours alone in my room facing a screen and a blank wall. But present with me always were the voices of all the Vietnamese people I knew and all the Vietnamese people I had encountered in movies and books. Always there for me were the voices of the Asian American writers who had come before, beginning in the late nineteenth century when they faced a level of incomprehension I can barely imagine. And always with me were the voices of those Asian Americans and other people of color whose political and social movements had broached the walls of racism and indifference and given me the chance to speak and be heard.

W. E. B. Du Bois's idea that Black people always see themselves through their own eyes and those of others helped me understand that I also experience that double consciousness, to some degree. I was an

American spying on my parents and a Vietnamese spying on Americans. But double consciousness is experienced not only through the gaze but also through the voice. I may speak for myself and only for myself, but I am perceived as speaking for others whether I like it or not, whether I want to or not. Instead of accepting this duality in which the so-called minority writer ventriloquizes the voiceless as their voice, I believe in two things: first, we all indeed have to find our own voices, but second, we must abolish the conditions of voicelessness.

For Asian Americans, even claiming an individual voice is fraught, for our place in the United States is to be the silent, acquiescent, apologetic model minority. We are neither expected to write nor to fight. We are not expected to speak alone, much less speak together. And yet, in the face of the anti-Asian violence that is perpetual in American society, routine in American warfare in Asia, and which resurged during the pandemic in the United States and many other countries, finding and claiming both our individual *and* collective voices is crucial. And here, what is powerful about literature and storytelling as art and as weapons is that they teach us how our otherness has been used to divide us and isolate us, and how our otherness can be used to draw us together.

Nevertheless, writing is for the most part a lonely act, where the otherness I have most often encountered is my own, and the otherness I have chosen not to think about exists within my own family. I think back to the opening lines of *The Woman Warrior:* "'You must not tell anyone,' my mother said, 'what I am about to tell you.'"[7] Kingston names the taboo and breaks it at the same time. In so doing, Kingston creates a parable of one of the writer's most important tasks, and that is to find what must not be told and tell it. But is this telling an act of honesty or betrayal? Sometimes telling the secret is both.

Just as otherness and voice are both matters of the collective and the individual, so is the secret. There are two kinds of secrets: the private secret and the open secret. The lure of the memoir as genre is to reveal the secret, whatever it happens to be, but in the context of the United States, or perhaps any country, the readerly demand is usually for the private secret: divorce, alienation, infidelity, mental illness, and the like. Like my mother's life. And her death.

Matters of the self, and only the self, not the collective, are the typical drama for an American storytelling world that honors showing over telling; that sneezes when politics nudges too close into fiction, poetry, movies, and television; that associates telling with the uncouth acts of writers who are barbarians. A lack of explicit politics *is* the politics of the dominant American literary world, leading many American writers to avoid certain open secrets. The open secret dares us to acknowledge its presence. The open secret of AMERICA™ is that white people founded it on genocide, slavery, war, and white supremacy, that orgy of blood born from colonization which continues staining the self and the other. The open secret of AMERICA™ is that we do not call colonization by its name. Instead, we give colonization another, more acceptable name: the AMERICAN DREAM™.

The title of the story I wrote about Má, "War Years," refutes how Americans and perhaps people the world over usually understand the lives of immigrants and refugees, burdened by private secrets as they chase the AMERICAN DREAM™. Understanding that this AMERICAN DREAM™ is actually the gold-plated brand name of American settler colonization, I portray Má's private secrets as shaped by the open secrets of colonization and wartime, a time in which I also live. A time in which everyone who inhabits our war machine lives.

In my mother's case, and mine, I find it impossible to separate private secrets from open secrets, my speaking for myself and my speaking for an other who includes my mother. A few years ago, after I had found one register of my voice in writing *The Sympathizer,* I reread the letter Kingston wrote me as well as the essays I wrote for her. I had remembered that I had written about my mother and the time she was committed to the Asian Pacific Psychiatric Ward at the Santa Clara Valley Medical Center. But I had remembered for decades writing about how that took place when I was a child. In rereading my essays for Kingston's class about my mother, I discovered what I had made myself forget, what

I had kept secret from myself: that in actuality my mother was in the Asian Pacific Psychiatric Ward when I was a college freshman, the year before I wrote my essay in 1991.

Back then, I wrote what my family—what my mother—would not have wanted me to say out loud, that "Someone out there—if not everyone—is trying to kill her. They crawl through the sewer and emerge through the toilet. She was waiting for them, locked in the bathroom, when my father decided enough was enough and knocked a hole in the door to reach her. It was my bathroom." Memory is odd, because I still do not remember the hole in my bathroom door, although I do remember the time my mother chased my father into the other bathroom, and when he locked himself inside, she smashed holes in that door with a chair. My father, normally fastidious about every detail, never repaired it. The gaping holes in the bathroom door revealed its hollowness for the rest of our years in that house.

But if I can remember that damaged door, I possess no image of sitting with my mother in the Asian Pacific Psychiatric Ward. My only record of that time was what I wrote: "She recognized me, but I was no more important in her world than the rest of the ugly furniture. She looked ahead at the opposite wall. Her mouth remained slightly open, her eyes slightly glazed, but she didn't move." The experience was so disturbing that I had to forget almost every aspect of it, including when it happened and my reaction to it. I also have no memory of this: "the tears started to come from me and I got up before anybody saw me crying, because nobody had seen me cry since the sixth grade. I walked into the bathroom without saying anything to her, but I don't think she noticed anyway. I locked myself in the bathroom stall, and my first sob made me gasp."

Má recovered and left the Asian Pacific Psychiatric Ward some weeks later, but if the experience was so unsettling that I had to write about it, it was also so unnerving that I had to forget about it until my mother died two days before Christmas Eve in 2018. By that time she had been ill for thirteen years, ever since suffering a relapse around

Christmas Eve in 2005 and returning to the Asian Pacific Psychiatric Ward for a second time. I did not take any notes this second time. I remember nothing of her second stay in the Asian Pacific Psychiatric Ward, even though I was thirty-four. Or if I do remember, I have kept it secret from myself.

If my mother was my first other, then she is also, as of now, my last other, not counting, perhaps, my self. Má was born in 1937 as Nguyễn Thị Bảy, her first name a number, seven, indicating her birth order. Her rural family was poor, and naming girls with numbers was common. She hated her first name, and when she became a US citizen, she changed it to Linda. She would not have wanted you to know that she barely had a grade school education, and that while I was reading *The Sound and the Fury*, she was reading the church newsletter, slowly, out loud, with the aid of a magnifying glass. There was no other reading material in our house besides my school books and library books. But I tell you this secret because even without much of an education, Má became a wealthy woman in Việt Nam, a self-made entrepreneur. She was determined to make something of herself, and when Việt Nam was divided in 1954, when she was seventeen, she fled south with her family, including her mother, and my father, her new husband. Then, when the communists caught up with her in 1975, she fled again to the United States, leaving behind her mother and sisters and adopted daughter. Having lost everything again, she rebuilt her life and wealth once more. Perhaps she did not have time to read, sacrificing her time instead so that her son could read, even as her son, diving deeper and deeper into English, turned himself into an other to his mother.

It took decades for me to understand what the costs of war were for my mother. For example, soon after we came to the United States as refugees, my mother's mother died. I was four years old. I vaguely remember sitting on steps, perhaps at the back of the house, with my father and brother. Something is being explained, but I do not understand it, this foreshadowing of what will come. One can see a foreshadow only from the future.

What happened was that Má had experienced her first breakdown and had gone to the hospital. My brother thinks the death of my mother's mother, so far away in Việt Nam, sent Má into a downward spiral from which she eventually resurfaced, only to be plunged again and again. Má came back, but I do not remember her return. She was simply present again. For the next sixteen years she would be who she always was, loving and supportive, hardworking and sacrificial, until she went to the Asian Pacific Psychiatric Ward when I was in college. Was the cause of my mother's illness a private secret, something to be found only in her mind and body? Or was the cause an open secret, history itself, which hammered on her repeatedly until it fractured her? Or was the cause both a private secret and an open secret?

Vietnamese people, how do you separate what is unique to you and your own personal trauma from war, colonization, the division and reunification of the country? From becoming a refugee or staying behind or being left behind? From being the child of refugees, soldiers, witnesses, survivors? From being the child of those who did not survive?

Vietnamese people, how do you separate yourself and your memories from History? Your private secrets from open secrets? Your self from your otherness? Your truth from your betrayal?

One more truth, one more betrayal when it comes to Má is that as unique as she was to me, she was not unique to others. Thousands of people lived lives as difficult, if not worse. Thousands lived lives as courageous, if not more so. Understanding this does not diminish my mother in any way. If anything, I understand Má better when I see her story against the backdrop of history. My mother, child of colonization and war. Me, grandchild of colonization and war. Also the child of Ba Má, who chose each other. For all that Má was lost to us for so many years, my father's love was not lost to her. I know because the last words Má says on her hospital bed in the family room before she says the Lord's Prayer with my father are for my father, to my father: *Em yêu anh.* This I will translate, even if the translation is not enough: I love you.

Then, the Lord's Prayer. Then, silence. My brother the doctor gives Má morphine while my sister-in-law the doctor watches. Má's breathing slows. I lean close to tell Má in Vietnamese that I love her. She lived a good life. A heroic life. A life that demanded so much strength, devotion, and love. I don't know where Má found those qualities. But I am the beneficiary.

Má gives no sign of hearing. Her breathing finally stops. It is midnight. Her journey on this earth, complete. When Ba asks me to close her eyes, I do so. Then he tells me to close her mouth. Her skin is already cold when I lift her jaw, and when I let it go, her mouth falls open again. Má has been silenced, but her voice will remain with me. Her mouth is open and I cannot close it.

When I remember Má, I hear her speak the mother tongue, which is also an other tongue, caressing me with the love and affection she bestowed on me throughout my childhood, giving me the confidence needed to portray her. And, in the end, betray her.

Did she ever forbid me from telling her story? No. I doubt she ever thought I would. She trusted me, who cannot trust my own memory. From this forgetfulness and unreliability, and from Má's journeys to the Asian Pacific Psychiatric Ward, where she was and was not herself, I have learned that the other is someone too close to us. So it is that my mother is mine and my mother is also other to me, as she was an other to herself.

As for me, a reluctant and unintentional memoirist, I have also learned that in telling on others, in speaking for others, the memoirist always tells upon himself as well, the one who is an other even to himself. What I tell myself is that Má loved me. Everything else I can forget.

3. ON PALESTINE AND ASIA

y mother was buried in a Californian cemetery, among many other Vietnamese refugees. When it came to national or racial identification, she called herself Vietnamese first and foremost, even though she had United States citizenship. Occasionally she might have considered herself Asian, and for a few years during my adolescence she and my father ran a small business called the Oriental Funding Corporation, a name that made me uneasy, although I did not know how to put it into words. She never called herself Asian American, which is the form of identification and otherness that initially politicized me and made it possible for me to think of myself as a writer, one with a genealogy and a cause.

Becoming and being an unapologetically Asian American writer led to some unexpected recognition and classification, as when I came across my books in BHV, a department store in the heart of Paris. There, in its bookstore, I found my books in French. The section under which my work was categorized? Anglo-Saxon literature. I felt no more Anglo-Saxon than I felt Oriental, but while I laughed at being included with the Anglo-Saxons, I would have been offended if my work was placed among Oriental or Asian literatures. I am Asian American, not Asian. As for Oriental, I can almost hear the sound of a gong when I say the word, not to mention smell the incense and feel a Persian rug under my necessarily bare feet. As Edward Said argued in *Orientalism,* the Oriental is an object and an opportunity manufactured by the Occident, a fantasy with very real consequences. What was an Oriental to me but a shadow to dispel, a double to destroy, a name to reject?

This is not merely a question about the politics of identity and culture, although it can be reduced to that, this great symbolic distinction between Anglo-Saxons and Orientals that a category like Asian American disrupts. If I had ended up in this Anglo-Saxon category in a French bookstore, it was ironically because I had written about and worked through what it meant to be Asian American, my particular brand of otherness, with its great possibilities and very serious limits. These limits have always been present in the Asian American category, and likely in many categories of collective identification that are based on solidarity of various kinds. Perhaps nothing so much as war reveals the contradictions and limits of solidarity.

Soon after I began delivering these Norton Lectures, Hamas launched its October 7 attack on Israel from its base in Gaza, killing approximately 1,200 Israelis, many of whom were civilians, many of whom were soldiers. Hamas seized 250 prisoners (the soldiers) and hostages (the civilians, including some who were not Israeli). In response, Israel launched a massive and vastly disproportionate campaign of bombing and ground assaults that destroyed much of Gaza, from homes to infrastructure, from schools to hospitals, and killed, as of this writing, at least 40,000 Palestinians, many of whom, perhaps the majority, were civilians and children. Israel also arrested at least nine thousand Palestinians, subjecting them to humiliation, abuse, torture, rape, and even death.[1]

The antiwar movement that erupted globally against Israel's war on Gaza was perhaps the most visible such movement since the opposition to the American war in Việt Nam. That movement has been met with concerted attempts by many Western governments and institutions to silence criticisms of Israel, the war, and Western support of Israel, ranging from arrests of protestors to the canceling of literary awards to writers to the firing of editors and university presidents. In such a situation, it was evident to me that it was necessary to speak out as vocally as I could against what I saw as an unjust war and occupation, one that was funded by billions of dollars in weapons and aid supplied by the United States, Israel's most important ally and the country of my citizenship.

Speaking out involved more than my personal conscience. I saw historical and political continuities between the American war in Việt Nam, which occurred when the United States chose to support France and its colonization of Việt Nam, and the American support of Israel's settler colonization. The United States is itself a settler colony, and the irony of being a refugee from an American war who earned his citizenship in such a colony is not lost on me. My belonging to the United States, as someone who is both insider and outsider, citizen and other, is made possible by the wars that have made the United States what it is. Becoming an Asian American for me was premised on wanting to belong to this country, particularly in opposition to the anti-Asian violence that has been endemic and systemic throughout the country's history and present. But what if the greatest acts of anti-Asian violence were not what was done to Asians once they arrived in the United States? What if the worst moments of anti-Asian violence were the wars of the United States in Asia? Or, as Said might call it, the Orient, in which he included Palestine.

Israel's war on Gaza should compel a response especially from Asian Americans, who have been called Oriental, and from any who have been classified or see themselves as other in some way, including writers, especially those who have sought to write through otherness. These responses to the war raise issues of self-defense, inclusion, and solidarity that have great meaning for anyone who has been classified as an other, including Asian American, Palestinian, Israeli, and Jewish writers—all of whom have grappled with what it means to be the monstrous other. For myself, as an Asian American writer radicalized partly by rejecting the label of the Oriental, Palestine should occupy an important place in my genealogy. But if Said's *Orientalism* provided much of the intellectual energy that drove the growth of Asian American literature and culture, many of us forgot or overlooked that Said was Palestinian and claimed the Palestinian cause. We Asian Americans appropriated his argument about Orientals, since his book did not, for the most part, deal with the Orient of the United States, found in Japan, China, Korea, the Philippines, Việt Nam, Cambodia, and Laos, which is to say East and Southeast Asia. Said addressed Europe's Orient, located in what Europeans called the Near East and Middle East, and which some writers and scholars with ancestry in those areas now call, in an act of renaming and reclaiming, West and Southwest Asia.

Orientalism appeared in 1978, four years after the publication of the most important anthology of Asian American literature, *Aiiieeeee!* The title comes from the death cries typically uttered by the Asian hordes killed by American firepower in American movies, which the anthology's four young editors—Frank Chin, Jeffery Paul Chan, Lawson Fusao Inada, and Shawn Wong—turned into their rallying cry. The *New York Times* favorably reviewed *Aiiieeeee!* and presciently singled out for praise Chan's short story "The Chinese in Haifa."[2] According to Shawn Wong, "many reviewers could only relate to Chan's story because it had Jewish characters in it. The story served as a cultural bridge to this brand-new thing called Asian American literature."[3]

Despite its impact at the time, the story has been mostly forgotten since, possibly because it raised an issue many Asian Americans did not want or know how to address: the significance of Israel and Palestine to Asian Americans. It is here, where Asian American literature and Jewish American representation meet over Israel and Palestine, that I will look at three key ways Asian Americans have organized ourselves, our politics, and our literature. In increasing order of difficulty, they are self-defense, inclusion, and solidarity. These three ways also resonate with others who have been subordinated, racialized, colonized, and so on.

Self-defense is needed to ward off efforts to kill and subjugate us, reducing us to the bare life of a human animal. In defending ourselves, we also author our own stories. But the danger in self-defense lies in becoming absorbed by our own victimization, and, through insisting so strenuously on our humanity, being incapable of acknowledging our inhumanity—or the humanity of our adversaries.

Through self-defense, we seek inclusion into a larger community that has excluded us, such as the nation. But if we succeed in gaining entry, we may forget who still remains excluded as an other, and whether we, the included, now participate in and profit from the mistreatment of others.

Inclusion requires solidarity, as those who have excluded others now extend hospitality to the excluded. The excluded also need solidarity as they seek kinship with each other. But how far does solidarity extend? A limited solidarity, defining selfhood narrowly, keeping circles of inclusion small and community identity uncontested, leads to the most acceptable politics and art in the eyes of dominant society. An expansive solidarity, wherein kinship grows between unlikely others in an ever-widening circle, is much more dangerous, both to dominant society and to ourselves.

These modes of self-defense, inclusion, and solidarity are all necessary, but also all double-edged. In the United States, these are the methods by which others have sought to become incontestably American. For Asian Americans, becoming American included a refusal to be Orientals. Finding that term demeaning, we named ourselves Asian Americans instead. Using this new name, Asian Americans wrote ourselves into being, seeking to save ourselves and the memory of our forebears from the forgetfulness of our descendants, the silences of our elders, and the violence, death, and erasure aimed at the Oriental. If the deaths of Orientals gave birth to Asian Americans, we in turn attempted to kill off the Oriental—symbolically if not literally.

The Oriental unsettles Asian Americans, but also disturbs the United States in even more profound ways today than either Asian Americans or even Asians can, as we see in "The Chinese in Haifa." Its protagonist is Bill Wong. Wong's wife has left him, and he is about to go fishing with his neighbor, Herb Greenberg. But on that morning Herb is upset because his mother is about to go to Haifa, the third-largest city in Israel, and the news has announced, in Herb's words, that "the Japs just bombed an Israeli airliner in Rome." This is based on a real attack by the Japanese Red Army in 1972 on Lod Airport, near Tel Aviv, which killed twenty-six people, Israelis as well as Christian pilgrims from Puerto Rico. "Goddamn Japs," Herb says, describing them as "three Japanese terrorists." Perplexed, Herb asks, "What in the hell do the Japs have against us?"

To Herb, Israel's existence is necessary for Jewish self-defense, and the Japanese attack is evidence of that need. Herb's plaintive question implies that Japs and Jews should have no shared antagonism. Bill, puzzled, says: "Japanese disguised as Arab guerrillas?" The shift from Japs to Japanese is Bill's deliberate refusal to use such racist language. The change from Herb's "terrorists" to Bill's "guerrillas" is also intentional, as is Bill's invocation of "Arab." Herb, however, ignores these shifts as well as Bill's confusion, which stems not just from hearing that Japanese in Rome killed people bound for Israel, but also over why Herb says "Japs" to his Chinese American friend. Instead, Herb insists, "They were Japs, dressed like Japs."[4]

When I first read this story as a college student, I had never heard of Japanese attacking Israelis, and I wondered why a collection of Asian American literature included a story about Chinese in Haifa. The anomalousness of the story, however, underscores the connection between Asian Americans and Jewish Americans as deviations from the American norm, two populations defending themselves against pervasive and enduring anti-Asian racism and antisemitism that are embedded in the American grain.

Both communities also foreground the need for inclusion. Jewish Americans have sought to become a part of the United States with great effectiveness if not total success, given the endurance of antisemitism. But in 1974, not quite three decades after World War II's end, Herb's Americanness might have felt as fragile as his Jewishness. As for Asian Americans, we are increasingly included in the United States, but our vulnerability to symbolic and actual violence remains, as evidenced by the surge in anti-Asian sentiment during the pandemic and the need, fifty years ago, to scream in protest.

"The Chinese in Haifa" recognizes similarities between Asian Americans and Jewish Americans, situated inside and outside of the United States and Americanness. The story moves toward a tentative solidarity between them. Herb's wife, Ethel, tells Herb's Haifa-bound mother, "Maybe you can find Bill a nice Jewish girl, Mama, in Haifa." Herb asks: "Are there Chinese in Haifa?" His mother says, "The Jews and the Chinese . . . they're the same. . . . You know there are Jews in China, there must be Chinese in Haifa. It's all the same, even in Los Angeles."[5]

That note of hopefulness belies the tragic, unspoken histories of the Chinese and Jewish diasporas. If Herb's unselfconscious racism mars that optimism, Bill responds in kind. He has been having an affair with Ethel, Herb's wife, and at the story's end, Bill has his own racist daydream as he imagines Herb dropping off his mother at the airport: "A vague collection of swarthy Japanese in mufti crowding around Herb's station wagon at the airport grew in [Bill's] mind's eye."[6] Someone normally in uniform is in mufti when they wear plain clothes, but a mufti is someone with legal expertise over Islamic religious matters. Is Bill fantasizing that Herb will be killed by pro-Islamic, antisemitic terrorists or guerrillas? Or is Bill sympathetic to Herb, who is about to be attacked by "swarthy Japanese" of the kind that once inflicted terrible atrocities against the Chinese?

The story provides no answer as to whether the attackers are terrorists or guerrillas, and gives no prescription as to whom one should feel solidarity with, or desire to be included with, as Herb and Bill each take stands of self-defense. The modes of self-defense, inclusion, and solidarity overlap, contradict, and potentially confuse—then and now. It is telling, for example, that Bill says "Arab" but never "Palestinian" or "Palestine," even though Palestinians trained the Japanese Red Army. His silence on Palestine foreshadows how Asian American consciousness will exclude Palestine, since Palestinians do not seem to be Asian. But

European Orientalism was transferred to the United States when it replaced Britain and France as the world's imperial power, and in the American imagination, Palestinians specifically, and Arabs and Muslims in general, are Oriental.

Said's afterword in *Orientalism* focused on these Orientals and their representations in the late 1970s. American representations of Arabs and Muslims depicted them mostly as terrorists, with the occasional chance to be good Orientals. The good other is willing to die for the West, while the bad other must be killed by the West. This dichotomy is central to how the Occident imagines its Orientals and the West its Asians, with the binary between good and bad others involving both anti-Asian racism and Western colonialism. In response to this racism, Asians and Orientals in the United States assembled under the inherently incoherent name of "Asian Americans."

The Asian American task of self-defense is made easier if we exclude the world outside the United States and the question of colonialism. Hence, "The Chinese in Haifa" would have been much more comforting if the Japanese terrorists or Arab guerrillas were removed. The result would be a more familiar tale about America's interethnic tensions and possibilities, about how the despised can despise each other yet learn to live together, whether as Chinese and Jewish American neighbors or as Asian Americans who can overlook the differences between being Chinese or Japanese. But Jeffery Paul Chan's insistence on referencing not only Jewish Americans but also Israelis and Arabs reveals that what happens inside the pluralistic society of the United States, often posed as a problem of race and racism, cannot be separated from war and colonialism.

For Asian Americans, the outside is Asia. We fear being associated with any part of Asia when that part clashes with the United States. World War II turned Japanese Americans into Japs, while the contemporary possibility of war with China has already provoked a surge of anti–Chinese American feeling that could quickly morph into anti–Asian American feeling. This fear underlies Bill Wong's uneasiness over Herb's use of "Japs" and about the possibility of being indiscriminately painted with an Oriental brush. Herb might feel the same, marked by Jewishness, Israel, and the threat of violence and death.

This sense of peril also provides a unifying experience for Asian Americans—a shared history exacerbated by our concern that most of the world does not know our nation's record of anti-Asian violence. This record includes lynchings, massacres, and brutal expulsions when white people felt there were too many of us in too close proximity; confinement to ghettos that white people sometimes burned down; laws preventing us from owning land, obtaining citizenship, or testifying in court, even as eyewitnesses to the murder of our friends by white people; government decrees preventing us from immigrating to this country, making the Chinese the first illegal immigrants in American history; signs saying "No Dogs or Filipinos Allowed"; ruthless exploitation of bodies and labor, from Chinese workers building the railroad to Japanese and Filipinos toiling in the fields to Asian women laboring in sweatshops. It includes the perpetual perception of Asian Americans as foreigners, the acceptability of anti-Asian jokes and slurs, and the routine murder and rape of Asians in American movies and television—all preparing the ground for the actual killing and raping of Asians and Asian Americans. Not least of all is our concern for the world's ignorance of America's wars in Asia, which killed millions of Asians, from the Philippine-American War of 1898 to the post–9 / 11 Forever War waged in Iraq (West Asia) and Afghanistan (Central Asia).

These deaths of Asians and Asian Americans, in the past and potentially in the future, ironically enable the lives of Asian Americans, bringing us together in our defiance. Creating literature was one of the most important ways we sought to shake off the Oriental double, defend ourselves, and fight for inclusion. Through literature, we give voice to our rightful place as Americans. However, as American power projected itself globally, Asian American literature became a subset of imperial literature. Is this why many of us are now silencing ourselves on the question of Palestine, because we are part of an imperial United States?

I was saved from being an Oriental when I encountered Asian American literature and politics in college. I was shocked to discover I knew nothing of Asian American history and its violence. Renaming myself as an Asian American, I became an activist at age nineteen, motivated by my tremendous conviction that Asian American literature and politics enabled us to seize control of our own stories from racist narratives that stripped us of humanity and subjected us to the terms of bare life: exclusion, imprisonment, exploitation, death. Our literature rattled the imagination, our movements shook society, each one clearing the way for the other.

As our populations and political power grew, so did our literature from its English-language origins in the late nineteenth century. Imagine our surprise a few years ago when the French newspaper *Le Monde* wrote on the success of Asian American literature in the early twenty-first century and used our name: *Asiatiques-Américains,* "Asian Americans." But if some of us managed to squeeze onto the great bookshelves of the West, perhaps it is because we are not apprehended—at the moment— as engaging in a hostile takeover. In France, those of Vietnamese descent are treated well, partly due to the perception that we work hard and desire inclusion but also partly because we are not Algerian, North African, Arab, Muslim, or Black, a situation parallel to the United States, where Asian Americans are who we are partly because of who we are not—Indigenous or Black.

In France as in the United States, the question of solidarity looms for those of Asian descent. By identifying with other Asians of different origins, we practice a solidarity aimed for inclusion. This solidarity was once radical, as people who fought one another during World War II— Chinese and Japanese, for example—came together. While this new-found similarity is important, if we settle for it and exclude those who still do not seem like us, it becomes limiting. The question is whether we can continually practice an expansive solidarity with others whom our country excludes, subordinates, and targets the most, both inside and outside our borders.

If Asian Americans decline expansive solidarity, we signal that we are not going to take over, that we know our place—that is, until we reach some unknown point when there are too many of us, as once upon a time there were also too many Jews in the Ivy League. A great comic novel in the manner of Philip Roth could be written about the plight of Asian Americans at Harvard or similar institutions and how these places embody power. The immigrant themes of aspiration, assimilation, and anxiety are present, the standard dilemmas of the ethnic nouveaux riches, from an earlier generation of Jewish Americans to their ethnic descendants, Asian Americans. Here as elsewhere, we foreground our success stories, which are inextricable from our sob stories. We are valedictorians, salutatorians, celebrities, influencers, actors, chefs, politicians, writers. We are your doctors, radiologists, internists, optometrists, dentists, pharmacists, nurses. We take your blood pressure, give you injections, empty your bedpans. We look into each and every part of you. We tutor you in math and play your classical music. We kneel at your feet to do your pedicures. We dry-clean your clothes. We introduced you to acupuncture and yoga and martial arts, but we have been so successful in these endeavors that we probably no longer teach you yoga or martial arts, since you like to teach them yourselves. We gave you an incredible array of spices, flavors, and dishes without which your lives, diets, and palates would be much blander. We design your microchips and program your code. We become the objects of your fantasies and desires. We smile and reassure you. We serve as your excuses to end affirmative action. We are your friendly competition. Until we are too much competition.

Words like *ethnic* and *immigrant* pad the hard foundations of enduring antisemitism and anti-Asian racism, as well as racialized and colonizing capitalism. To speak of capitalism without racism or colonialism exiles their embarrassing necessity in the same way that some can forget how enslavement, genocide, and exploitation enriched the

West. Joseph Conrad, in *Heart of Darkness,* described the colonizers' process of enrichment: "They were conquerors, and for that you want only brute force . . . your strength . . . just an accident arising from the weakness of others. They grabbed what they could get for the sake of what was to be got . . . robbery with violence, aggravated murder on a great scale."[7] Imperial conquest created the mass migration of fearful and hopeful Asians to the United States, where they encountered anti-Asian violence. The novelist Julie Otsuka described the danger that other Americans saw in the Japanese immigrants of the early twentieth century: "We were an unbeatable, unstoppable economic machine and if our progress was not checked the entire western United States would soon become the next Asiatic outpost and colony."[8] How, then, to stop our progress? In the Japanese American case, through the incarceration camp, which demonstrated the arbitrariness of the law and how the state could take away rights and lives at any time.

Anti-Asian violence and the deaths of both Asians and Asian Americans is a dominant theme in Asian American literature, providing the basis for singular sorrows but also more capacious grief, *if* we think about how we relate to others subjected to similar violence, how our Asian Americanness would not be possible without the land taken from Indigenous and colonized peoples. Our contradiction is exacerbated by the following problem: if the Oriental is a monstrosity, is our reviving it and renaming it the Asian American any less monstrous? Japanese, Chinese, Koreans, and Filipinos would never have called themselves "Asian" until they came to the United States. When these different parts could speak to each other in English, the Asian American body became animated. As that body grew, and as its capacity for speech became ever more vigorous, that body with its new name no longer seemed so ridiculous to other people and, most importantly, to Asian Americans themselves, as well as to those who had not yet heeded the call to become Asian American.

In the wake of the war in the former Indochina, those who sought self-defense, inclusion, and solidarity as Asian Americans included

Vietnamese, Cambodian, Laotian, Hmong, Thai, Indonesian, Malaysian, and Burmese. Along with East Asians who migrated before them, these Southeast Asians experienced European and American interventions into their countries via war and colonialism, and similar anti-Asian treatment upon reaching the United States. Overseas colonialism and domestic racism have also compelled South Asian immigrants from India, Pakistan, Bangladesh, Nepal, and more to say that they are Asian Americans too. That self-recognition—that willingness to take on a name—is the difference between being labeled Oriental or Asian against one's will, versus seeking identification as an Asian American.

This identification with a group is self-defense. Self-defense can lead to a politics based on identity and the demand for inclusion, as well as asking for equity, for our fair share in representation and democracy, capitalism and the military-industrial complex. But this desire for identification can also lead far beyond the mere demand for inclusion, to a politics of expansive solidarity across seemingly huge differences. The incoherence of Asian America lies in the gap between the acceptable politics of limited solidarity and the potentially more radical politics of expansive solidarity. To be included, Asian Americans have to contain ourselves, daub on the makeup of assimilation to hide our seams and our monstrousness, learn what is acceptable to do and say and what is not. But to engage in a politics and a literature of expansive solidarity requires opening the self to others and saying what should not be said.

Here, the silence of "The Chinese in Haifa" on Palestine matters. It points toward the Asian American ambivalence about how far Asia or the Orient extends, which is to say how far self-defense, inclusion, and solidarity extends—and to whom. Asia is the world's largest continent, extending from Turkey to the west and Japan to the east, from Kazakhstan to the north and Sri Lanka to the south and Indonesia to the southeast. Israel and Palestine are in Southwest Asia. The geography opens a critical question: what if they, Israelis or Palestinians, identified as Asian and, eventually, migrated to the United States, as Asian American? If the question seems absurd, that is because claiming affiliation via Asia or the Orient itself, so enormous and heterogeneous, might already seem absurd. And yet the absurdity has been outweighed by the tragedies of racism and colonialism, which have driven numerous people and their descendants from one corner of Asia to ally with people and descendants of an opposite corner. Are these alliances any more absurd, or less tragic, than the Jews and the Chinese of Los Angeles, of Haifa, of China, finding common ground?

Self-defense, inclusion, and solidarity are not mutually exclusive or linear stages of becoming Asian American or some other kind of other. They exist simultaneously as different, sometimes conflicting impulses. For Asian Americans, these conflicting impulses mean that we recognize Pacific Islanders and Native Hawaiians as part of our necessary coalition, even if they are not Asian American. But the existence and survival of Kānaka Maoli, CHamoru, and Samoans should trouble Asian Americans, and Americans as a whole, reminding the United States itself that it is a settler colonial country violently assembled through conquest, in this case of numerous Pacific Islands and Hawaii. The outside of colonialism is already inside the United States and inside Asian American communities, unsettling our desire to settle. The more American we become, the more we may affirm this country's settler colonialism with our silence about how we can be citizens and colonizers at the same time. The condition of our belonging, our inclusion, is our silence.

"The Chinese in Haifa" tentatively brings up colonization by mentioning "Arab guerrillas." Guerrillas must be fighting against something, and this revolt of Arab guerrillas disrupts the antiracist consensus that brings Asian Americans and Jewish Americans together, a unity that renders Palestinians invisible and inaudible. The ultimate silencing is death, with American support of Israel inextricable from the deaths of Palestinians, the poet Mahmoud Darwish argues in *Memory for Forgetfulness,* his memoir set during the Israeli siege and bombardment of Beirut in 1982. Darwish says of Palestinians that "America still needs us a little. Needs us to concede the legitimacy of our killing. Needs us to commit suicide for her, in front of her, for her sake."[9] Describing the

Israeli shelling of Beirut, Darwish could be narrating the Israeli attack on Gaza forty-one years later: "I don't want to die disfigured under the rubble. I want to be hit in the middle of the street by a shell, suddenly."[10]

Given the silence around Palestine in "The Chinese in Haifa," it is fitting that Darwish brings up Haifa at his memoir's end. Haifa, which he calls the Dove, is a city from which most of the Arab population was expelled by Jewish forces in 1948. Haifa symbolizes all that was lost, so much so that one Palestinian fisherman in Darwish's telling attempts to return by rowing a boat from Beirut to Haifa. "A week later, the sea brought his body back to the coast of Tyre, back to the rock where he used to gaze at the Dove."[11] In another story, Darwish asks a fellow Palestinian where he hails from. "Haifa," the man says.[12] But: "I wasn't born there. I was born here, in the refugee camp."[13] To be from somewhere but not born there describes an exile that descends generationally, leading to an existence, Darwish says, "In a middle region between life and death."[14] Caught in this zone, Darwish concludes his memoir by saying, "I don't see a dove."[15] Haifa is beyond reach or sight, as is everything else a dove might symbolize.

Expansive solidarity might help rescue us from the sadness and despair found in Darwish's memoir. I end with two writers who embrace expansive solidarity as they deal with Israel and Palestine. In Nadine Gordimer's *Writing and Being,* she describes being an other in her own country, apartheid-era South Africa—a feeling of alienation inseparable from the isolation of becoming a writer. Having rejected apartheid and her own implication in it, Gordimer criticized her white-ruled society, a stance complicated by being the daughter of European Jewish immigrants. Consider, Gordimer asks, how immigrants such as her parents could come to South Africa while opening a store serving a community of Black miners. A generation later, the immigrants and their children have become upwardly mobile and moved on. But the Black miners remain where they are. The problem, Gordimer understood, was one of racism and settler colonization, both of which enabled her and her immigrant parents to profit, their Jewishness offset by whiteness.

Gordimer invokes Amos Oz of Israel as another writer critical of his own society. She focuses on his novel *Fima,* whose titular character she describes as carrying "both the embittered history, millennia of persecution, of the Jewish people, and the embittered history of their Occupation by conquest of land belonging to another people, the Palestinian Arabs."[16] Despite having written this thirty years ago, the words of both Gordimer and Oz are still depressingly relevant. Oz depicts Fima, an outlier among his fellow Israelis, saying, "We're the Cossacks now, and the Arabs are the victims of the pogroms."[17] Fima continues: "Can a worthless man like me have sunk so low as to make a distinction between the intolerable killing of children and the not-so-intolerable killing of children?"[18] In one charged, symbolic moment, Fima comes across a cockroach in his kitchen and raises his shoe to smash it. But while examining the cockroach, "he was filled with awe at the precise, minute artistry of this creature, which no longer seemed abhorrent but wonderfully perfect; a representative of a hated race." He leaves the cockroach alone. For Gordimer, "the hated race, persecuted and confined, is Fima's own. He is himself the cockroach; and so are the blacks, and at his moment in history, in the Occupied Territories, the Palestinians. And he himself . . . is the hater, the persecutor, the one with the hammer, the raised shoe."[19]

Human and inhuman. Victim and victimizer. Expansive solidarity helps us recognize that we can be both in turn—even at the same moment. From defending one's self and demanding inclusion for people like one's self, one should then be able to recognize the demands of others who are excluded or who are under attack, and from there, heed the call for solidarity. One should. That does not mean one can or one does. Gordimer did and published her book in 1995 on a quietly triumphal note: the struggle against apartheid had won, and she could finally claim her country as her own. For her, inclusion could only be achieved by ending apartheid and settler colonialism rather than agreeing to them; otherwise, inclusion entailed an erosion of one's soul and art. Gordimer's expansive, radical solidarity is actually a defense of the self—her own self and the ethical, political, and artistic integrity needed to be a writer of her kind.

I return to my own otherness. Being Asian American is not the only dimension of myself. It is just one aspect, born from defending myself and others seen like me. I cease being an Asian American if and when Asian Americans cannot emerge from self-defense, inclusion, and a limited solidarity bound by race and nation in order to embrace an expansive, global solidarity. My Asian Americanness matters less than my ethics, politics, and art. Together they constitute a repository of a stubborn otherness that resists the lure of a domesticated otherness satiated by belonging. For Asian Americans, inclusion is crucial but complicated when it means belonging to a settler and imperial country that promotes the colonization and occupation of other lands. What is the worth of defending our lives if we do not seek to protect the lives of others? As for whom we should feel solidarity with, the answer is simple, albeit difficult: whoever is the cockroach. Whoever is the monster.

4. ON CROSSING BORDERS

My father has crossed many borders. Born in northern Việt Nam under French rule in 1933, he was educated in a French Catholic school. More than eighty years later, a widower, he could still sing fragments of French songs when we sat together at the dining table. The meal I could prepare which he most enjoyed was filet mignon, medium rare, with a glass of red wine. He had a cupboard full of Louis Jadot Beaujolais, for when he liked something, he bought it in bulk. When he stopped being able to eat meat and drink wine, I took the last two bottles of Louis Jadot and brought them home with me, where they remain untouched. Perhaps I will drink one when he passes away. Perhaps I will open the second decades from now and see what I remember when I taste it, even if all I will taste is spoilt wine.

By then, my father will have long ago passed across the last border any of us will see. I know of at least two other borders that he crossed during his life. In 1954, as a newlywed at twenty-one with his seventeen-year-old wife, my father left his childhood home and moved south across the border, where Việt Nam had been partitioned into a communist north and anticommunist south following the defeat of French colonizers by Vietnamese revolutionaries. My mother's entire family chose to leave the north, along with 800,000 other Vietnamese Catholics fearing communist persecution. My father's family chose to stay, so my father left behind his parents, his younger sister, and three younger brothers. He would not see them again for forty years. Ulysses was away from home for only twenty years. Does my father's journey away from home and back to it four decades later deserve the name of an epic? If not, what form should my father's story take?

The question of form and its relationship to a life lived interests me as a writer and as a border crosser, as my father's son and as a father myself. A half century years after my father left his childhood home, I visited the compound. My aunt had married and moved out long ago, but my three paternal uncles still lived there, along with many of their children and grandchildren. From my youth until my visit and past then until the present, my parents have sent home money to the relatives every year to help them survive. On this visit, I gave all the adults envelopes of cash, the amounts determined by my father, and thought about what my life would have been like if my parents had never left in 1954, or in 1975, when they fled from Sài Gòn and crossed yet another border to the United States. If I am inclined to see the journeys of my parents as heroic, the writer Amitava Kumar pushes back against the praise for those who cross borders: the immigrants, the refugees, the undocumented, the expatriates, the tourists, the settlers, the conquerors. He writes that "it is not the immigrant but the ones who stay behind who are the true unvanquished."[1]

It is safe to say that perceptions of migrants are contradictory. In their countries of origin, they are sometimes celebrated for having embarked on adventures and sometimes criticized as having abandoned their homes. In the countries of their arrival, they can appear as terrifying threats in another people's history or be welcomed as fresh blood. If they face hostility and suspicion, migrants might feel the need to insert themselves into their new nation's chronicles of conquest. The migrant's heroism can then harmonize with their host nation's self-image, as well as affirming that nation's hospitality and generosity.

This is what happens in Jhumpa Lahiri's short story "The Third and Final Continent," from her lauded collection *The Interpreter of Maladies,* which focuses on Indian immigrants to the United States. I admire the formal elegance of much of Lahiri's writing, especially her short stories, a genre in which she excels and in which I am at my most miserable. I spent seventeen horrible years writing short stories on a similar theme as Lahiri's, signaled by the title of my book: *The Refugees.* The book frustrated me because I did not understand, intuitively, the genre of the short story, where, generally speaking, less is more. Almost every single moment of writing the stories agonized me, and I am just fortunate that as a masochist and a Catholic, I enjoyed the suffering.

Whether or not Lahiri suffered in writing her book, her stories themselves appear effortless. Part of that gracefulness stems not just from the art of her writing, but its ideology, at least as it is manifest in *The Interpreter of Maladies.* The shape of her thinking about being an immigrant and an American fits seamlessly with both the streamlined qualities of a realistic short story and with how many Americans like to imagine their country, its hospitality, and its audaciousness. So long as the migrant comes to conquer the United States figuratively, by participating in our collective mythology of limitless capitalist progress into a democratic utopia with an SUV in every garage, the migrant is often, if not always, welcome. In "The Third and Final Continent," Lahiri captures the quotidian odyssey of this kind of migrant and the way his story illuminates the shadow-free national epic of the United States as a land of innocents pursuing happiness.

A young Indian graduate student has arrived in 1960s Boston after a short stay in London. The United States is his third and last continent. He rents a room from an elderly widow who was born during the Civil War. Despite her age and connection to a time of racial and national horror, she welcomes this Indian immigrant and, when his Indian fiancée arrives, welcomes her as well, blessing the start of an Indian American family who will be part of a new, nonwhite generation. One arc of the narrative is about progress past the country's racial sins. The other narrative arc concerns heroism, for Neil Armstrong lands on the moon during the Indian student's time in the widow's house. Decades later, as a happily married American citizen with successful sons, the narrator reflects on his American life via the moon landing:

> While the astronauts, heroes forever, spent mere hours on the moon, I have remained in this new world for nearly thirty years. I know that my achievement is quite ordinary. I am not the only man to seek his fortune far from home, and certainly I am not the first. Still, there are times I am bewildered by each mile I have traveled, each meal I have eaten, each person I have known, each room in which I have slept. As ordinary as it all appears, there are times when it is beyond my imagination.[2]

When I look at my father, who no longer recognizes me, I wonder if his accomplishments bewilder him. Lahiri's understatedly heroic immigrant template attracts me, with my desire to see my father as a bold voyager whose achievement parallels those of the astronauts. If Neil Armstrong became the ideal for the nation and of the nation, then so does the immigrant in his own quiet, anonymous manner, his story resonant with a nation he has come to accept.

Armstrong's story comforts in another manner: he survives and returns home. What of the migrant who does not survive or who does not return? The American mythology of immigration is perhaps too life- and nation-affirming to consider migration as an experience of death or exile, a condition from which one cannot return and where one does not feel truly at home. The writer Ha Jin, in his book *The Writer as Migrant,* argues that "the most significant literature dealing with human migration has been written on the experience of exile. By contrast, immigration is a minor theme, primarily American. Therefore, a major challenge for writers of the immigrant experience is how to treat this subject in response to the greater literary traditions."[3] My father is not an immigrant but a refugee, whose experience is closer to exile, especially if we consider how exiles typically die far from their homelands. My father has now spent more of his life here than there. He expressed his commitment to this country when he bought burial plots for himself and my mother in that California cemetery where she now rests. That burial plot, he told me years later, was a great investment. What cost three thousand dollars then is worth more than twenty thousand dollars today. In AMERICA™, even death makes for smart investment and real estate opportunities.

While capitalism has helped to shape the form of my father's eventual passing, so too has Vietnamese Catholicism. Vietnamese Catholic death rituals involve a viewing from morning to evening, a mass with biblical readings and choir hymns, the scent of incense, the chanting of prayers, the burial itself. My father has planned every last detail of his departure, and oversaw this form for my mother when she passed away five years ago. The ceremony was executed so perfectly that my father-in-law said he wanted something of equal quality, a wish his daughters granted when he passed away last year. The repetition of the form of mourning comforts the living as we contemplate our final exit. I grew up with a deep sense of this, for every night in childhood, I encountered the scene of my parents seated on the couch in a dim living room praying the rosary together in a language I only poorly understood, facing a wall furnished with a crucifix and pictures of a white Jesus and Mary. My parents were between two worlds that were alien to me—Việt Nam, in the past, and the afterlife, in the future. The afterlife was bright, but death was a continent from whose depths the explorers never returned. The ones who clinically died and came back to life saw only the shores of death.

The only other returnees are ghosts, who may really exist but do not usually appear in realist literature. The immigrant literature of realism—of which Lahiri's story is an exemplar, both for its artistic and personal grace, as well as its deep love for the immigrant as intrepid traveler—often forestalls, occludes, hedges on death and the final border crossing into the ultimate otherness. While Lahiri's immigrant does not mention death as the actual final continent and destination of everyone's last journey, death certainly does appear in a great deal of this realistic literature, from the ends of individuals due to personal circumstances and the demise of many from various ghastly calamities. But the realism of the literature insulates readers somewhat from the incomprehensibility of death, both of the personal and collective kinds. In Lahiri's story, for example, not only is the future death of our immigrant narrator forestalled, even in his old age, but so is the death of his landlady. By the end of the story, she has conveniently disappeared, along with the Civil War history from which she emerged.

The seamlessness of effective realism serves as a buffer against the emotions generated in those who die, those who witness and remember the death of others, and those who seek to recover the deaths for which they themselves were not present. How can realism adequately confront something so unreal as the final undoing? Death was not merely abstract to me as a child—it was unreal, unimaginable, unknowable. The story of the immigrant arriving as a stranger in a strange land, who then becomes a part of that land, affirms life, not death. But if we imagine immigrants as heroic, we should ask why. What did they escape? Was it, perhaps, mass death, or premature death, due to forces beyond their control? And if the ones who stayed were also heroic and unvanquished, was it because they confronted these conditions of mass or premature death? By celebrating the courage of migrants, do we foreground their accomplishments in order to obscure, in some cases, how our interventions as a country required them to be brave in order to survive? And what of all those who failed to survive?

The poet Ken Chen has also approached the issue of death and his father through what he calls "migration surrealism." In his text "I Was Ostensibly Searching For My Father, But.," he descends into the "underworld" in order to find his departed father.[4] Instead of imagining the abyss, he finds himself "trying to recuperate my right to hallucinate." Hallucination is the right response to the scale of death and its terrors for so many who have reached the infernal regions through "Death as migration." The dead he hallucinates died when they stayed at home, or died when they traveled, but died because of forces beyond their control that rendered their staying or their departure heroic, in the eyes of some. Some of those forces were unleashed by colonizers and conquerors for whom borders mattered not—at least the borders of others, always open, ready to be transgressed, versus their own borders, which were to be defended.

The continent of death has no guards, however. All are welcome, and, like Orpheus, Chen wanders into the underworld, seeing

> everything that ever died. I saw the beginning, the true beginning, the beginning of modern capitalism . . . I saw that the beginning had twin poles: in the New World, where the indigenous people fled the conquering hordes, strange men who would casually behead the people they encountered and set their hounds to tear the flesh of infants, and in the west coast of Africa, where there came a story that these traders of strange cargo must be cannibals, piling up as they did colossal mounds of bones, whitening in the sun. I saw men in India strapping the bodies of insurrectionary sepoys to the mouths of cannons. And there was the Congo, where I saw the West come carrying bags of hands. They had taken the hands from the people who lived there. In My Lai, was it ears? What was it in Malaya? . . . Listing these horrors in such a casual way—it shames one to write it, shames one to read it. How then to represent what I have come to call sublime trauma, the absolute terror of colonialism that is too gargantuan to be represented, words whose monument deforms our mouths as we speak them, events too much almost to even bear glimpsing?

If the language and form of realism is insufficient for grasping the scope of the underworld, the mythology of the heroic traveler is also not enough, for in elevating the individual this mythology cannot address the scale of collective conquest and death, resistance and survival.

Secular and religious epics might be better, being decidedly unrealistic, even hallucinogenic, as with the Bible. This particular holy book is replete with fantastic tales of exile, migration, and displacement, beginning with Adam and Eve, refugees from the garden of Eden who have bequeathed their Christian descendants with a perpetual nostalgia for the lost land of innocence from which they have been exiled. Then there is Noah, cast afloat in a mass extinction event, repopulating the world with his living cargo. Isn't his ark a boat for the very first boat people? This is why, in my novel *The Committed,* the rickety boat with which my band of Vietnamese refugees flees Việt Nam is described as an "ark," finding itself on a "wine-dark sea," in allusion to Homer's *Odyssey.*

In epics and fables from the Bible to Greek mythology, the hero can cross the last border and return from the dead. Realism is not required, and even contradicts the promises and lures of these kinds of stories, which involve a reversal of time. We mere mortals go from birth to death, but resurrection exists in divine time and implies what Chen calls "Death as time travel." I gestured at how the migrant also travels in time in my novel *The Sympathizer,* which I did not think of as a realistic work but rather a European modernist version of the Great American Novel, or maybe just a debased refugee knockoff. Against the linear optimism of American mythmaking, the narrator of my Not So Great American Novel, a refugee and a spy, enters the United States on a mission of sabotage rather than patriotic affirmation. In the land of plenty, he sees a clock on the wall of a Vietnamese restaurant

carved from hardwood into the shape of our homeland. For this clock that was a country, and this country that was a clock, the minute and hour hands pivoted in the south, the numbers of the dial a halo around Saigon. Some craftsman in exile had understood that this was exactly the timepiece his refugee countrymen desired. We were displaced persons, but it was time more than space that defined us. While the distance to return to our lost country was far but finite, the number of years it would take to close that distance was potentially infinite. Thus, for displaced people, the first question was always about time: When can I return? ... Refugee, exile, immigrant—whatever species of displaced human we were, we did not simply live in two cultures, as celebrants of the great American melting pot imagined. Displaced people also lived in two time zones, the here and the there, the present and the past, being as we were reluctant time travelers. But while science fiction imagined time travelers as moving forward or backward in time, this timepiece demonstrated a different chronology. The open secret of the clock, naked for all to see, was that we were only going in circles.[5]

As a child, I saw that clock hanging in more than one Vietnamese restaurant in San José, where Vietnamese refugees engaged in Proustian moments over bowls of phở. Could realism capture the malaise of homesickness that plagued some migrants? Can realism show me what whirls inside my father's head as he approaches the final border?

Perhaps, but my sense that realist linearity might not be sufficient in telling all the stories of migrants, border-crossers, and my father led me to writers who have dealt with memory by foregrounding the act of remembering itself, and how remembering shapes and perhaps distorts reality. For *The Sympathizer,* I was interested in memory's density, so I drew on writers fascinated by memory and who exhibited a particular richness of prose and style, from Toni Morrison to Maxine Hong Kingston, from António Lobo Antunes to W. G. Sebald. For *A Man of Two Faces,* I thought about how my existence as person and writer was possible because history had blown up Việt Nam and scattered millions of its people all over the world. Since memory could be a jagged assembly of shards as much as a thick stream of consciousness, I sought a style even more fragmentary, circular, and occasionally feverish for this blend of memoir, history, and memorialization.

Some books that have influenced me are difficult to classify, in the way migrants can be hard to classify, in transit between nation-states with enforced borders. Genres and styles have borders too, which is why conventional realism, with its clear boundaries marking how fiction should and should not look, suits immigrant narratives that affirm national identities. Nationalism and realism mold both citizens and immigrants, the latter into being or becoming knowable others. But what if the migrant is unknowable, someone who threatens national identities and borders? The violence of partition, of borders being changed by forces beyond the migrant's control, may lead these anomalies to question the very foundation of the nation-state, and persuades some writers who deal with unknowable others to be skeptical of realism itself.

Gloria Anzaldúa's *Borderlands / La Frontera* is situated on the US-Mexico border, a line established by the American conquest of what was once the northern half of Mexico. Anzaldúa calls herself "a member of a colonized people in our own territory."[6] Mixing prose and poetry, memoir and criticism, the theoretical and the spiritual, the personal and political, and English and Spanish, often untranslated, she describes the border as a

> 1,950 mile-long open wound
> dividing a *pueblo,* a culture
> running down the length of my body,
> staking fence rods in my flesh
> splits me   splits me
> *me raja   me raja*
> This is my home
> this thin edge of
> barbwire.[7]

While Lahiri's Indian immigrant identifies with the heroic nation and its space-exploring heroes, Anzaldúa stands with and on the tense, potentially violent southern border that defines the nation-state, preventing people from moving freely. If Lahiri's Indian immigrant establishes a family as a claim to the nation, enabling his family and the national family to merge seamlessly, Anzaldúa reminds us that both the nation and the family can abuse those who do not fit in.

For Anzaldúa, national borders are reinforced by borders between languages and religions, genders and sexualities. These human borders contrast with "the skin of the earth," which is "seamless," and the sea, which "cannot be fenced."[8] Anzaldúa sees herself as part of nature and counts herself among the border crossers, whom she describes as "the squint-eyed, the perverse, the queer, the troublesome, the mongrel, the mulato, the half-breed, the half dead"—in short, the less than human and the nonnormal who threaten both the conventional family and the nation that envisions itself through that family.[9] The geographical border makes very visible, with actual walls and real barbwire, what is true for so many other borders. Anzaldúa's claim is that one can cut through that barbwire, and turn the border into the cutting edge.

Theresa Cha's *Dictee* pushes this cutting edge. The book is a strange, compelling, unclassifiable work of enormous, unruly, unrealistic aesthetic ambition. Cha was born in South Korea two years before the 1953 armistice that ended the Korean War for the United States but not for Koreans, who remain divided into two countries facing off over the demilitarized zone. After migrating to the United States during the Cold War, which certainly was not cold for the approximately two million Koreans who died in the war, Cha studied film theory and became an experimental filmmaker at the University of California, Berkeley, where, a decade later, I studied her work, including her mystifying and unforgettable short films. Cha was educated in English, Korean, and French, all three languages appearing in *Dictee,* along with Chinese and Latin. Despite her multilingualism, Cha emphasizes a halting relationship to language: "Broken speech . . . Cracked tongue. Broken tongue. Pidgeon. Semblance of speech."[10]

Dictee can be understood as a broken mold, leaving behind shards of a shattered self in juxtaposed fragments of letters, found documents, photographs, film stills, enigmatic images, mysterious movies. There are evocations of Greek mythology and muses, the Japanese colonization of Korea, the martyrdom of Joan of Arc and the teenage patriot Yu Guan Soon, the patriarchy and rituals of Catholicism, and dictation and translation exercises between French and English. Writing from the position of a shattered self who cannot be classified, she composes a list of questions that might be directed at such an anomaly:

What nationality
or what kindred and relation
what blood relation
what blood ties of blood
what ancestry
what race generation
what house clan tribe stock strain
what lineage extraction
what breed sect gender denomination caste
what stray ejection misplaced

She concludes with a response that mixes Latin and English:

Tertium Quid neither one thing nor the other[11]

Being neither one nor the other could apply to Cha herself or her mother, who grew up under Korean colonialism and immigrated to the United States. Cha depicts her mother's life as epic and historic, interwoven with Korea's twentieth-century tragedies. When her mother finally returns to Korea late in life, however, she finds neither the heroic opportunity to be a Ulysses, recovering her home, nor a sentimental chance at wholeness and healing. Instead, "You return and you are not one of them . . . the papers give you away . . . They ask you identity. They comment on your inability or ability to speak. Whether you are telling the truth or not about your nationality."[12] This interrogation by border guards shows how violence against the unclassifiable, anomalous other can be linguistic, symbolic, and discursive, as when Japanese colonizers forced Koreans like Cha's mother to speak Japanese. This violence can also manifest in invasion, war, and colonization, when a people exults in "the suffering institutionalized on another ... one enemy nation has disregarded the humanity of another."[13]

The nation can also aim this violence within, as when soldiers and police massacre students engaged in antigovernment protests. In the us versus them world of harsh nationalism, these student rebels had become unknowable others, neither one thing nor the other. Lahiri's patriotic immigrant stands in contrast. Realism, a reassuring literary form, posits this immigrant as a knowable other fitting the mold, reassuring the nation rather than terrorizing it like the unknowable other threatens to do. Like Anzaldúa and Cha, I am more attracted to this kind of other, perhaps because unknowability comes closer to the enigma and danger of the writing process, approximating the fear a writer feels about unlocking what hides inside. Both *Borderlands / La Frontera* and *Dictee* are accounts of narrators becoming writers, with Anzaldúa finding what she calls her "wild tongue," while Cha writes of her narrator, who might be herself, that *"She says to herself if she were able to write she could continue to live."*[14]

Perhaps living through writing motivates my final example of a border crosser who courted death and resisted realism: Behrouz Boochani, author of the memoir *No Friend But the Mountains*. A Kurd from Iran, a self-described "child of war," Boochani flees Iran due to repression of the Kurdish people and their movement for an independent Kurdistan.[15] He embarks on what he calls an "odyssey": a perilous three-month journey by land, to Indonesia, and a more hazardous voyage by sea, aiming for Australia.[16] "Getting on any one of those boats is an extraordinary risk ... It is truly a battle against death."[17] Boochani understands his journey as a mythic one, writing his account as epic and allegory mixed with poetry. Seeing himself and his fellow travelers are not so much individuals as types because the authorities they encounter treat them as stereotypes, he bestows epithets instead of birth names on his companions: the Cadaver, the Insomniac, the Cow, the Giant, the Prophet, the Comedian, the Hero, all facing existential questions of life and death, courage and humanity.

The Australian government intercepts the boat and exiles the refugees to Papua New Guinea's Manus Island, "in the middle of the ocean," among inhabitants that Australian officials see as "savage" and "cannibals" but whom Boochani, as a Kurd, sees as fellow Indigenous people.[18] This island exile evokes *Robinson Crusoe,* except with masses of refugees as antiheroic castaways instead of Daniel Defoe's titular, singular hero. The story becomes a prison diary, full of awful experiences that he narrates as hallucinations. Boochani finds himself in "a prison of filth and heat," a "zoo full of animals of different colours and scents," where the refugees are given numbers, strip searched, monitored even in the toilets, kept in cages, and given ill-fitting clothes that "transform our bodies . . . [and] utterly degrade us."[19] The list of humiliations, from disgusting toilets to a diet bordering on starvation, reduces the refugees to Anzaldúa's "half dead" and pressures them to seek voluntary deportation.[20]

In the face of such degradations, prison diaries or memoirs are often narratives of resistance, self-transformation, and rebirth, given that the prisoners have become writers through their incarceration. Prisons are where states keep official and unofficial enemies, including writers, with the Australian government regarding refugees as "the enemy" invading by boat.[21] For Boochani, the prisoners are "captured soldiers," "prisoners of war" and "sacrificial subjects of violence."[22] They are also "hostages," Boochani says, "made examples to strike fear into others, to scare people so they won't come to Australia."[23] He wavers between feeling "crushed" and "worthless," and being the "person who conquered this great expanse of ocean on a rotting boat . . . I feel a kind of victory . . . I can erase all the sinking feelings . . . [and] replace them with hope and joy."[24] By the end, the hostages rebel and seize the prison, some at the cost of their own lives. Although Papua New Guinea declared the prison illegal in 2016, Boochani remained there, as unaware of his fate at the conclusion of his narrative as a character from Kafka, Camus, or Beckett— fitting for an existential drama.[25]

But just as Anzaldúa and Cha mix discourses, so do Boochani and his translator Omid Tofighian, who use theory and criticism in an important afterword that serves as the real ending for the book. This afterword frames the reading of the book and suggests that refugees are not only objects of study, but also potentially critics. Their prison is not only a site of punishment and mortification but a school where some refugees can teach themselves and learn to theorize their own existence. "What is a border?" Boochani asks after his informal prison education. "My whole life has been impacted by this concept of 'border.'"[26] While Lahiri's law-abiding immigrant accepts the existence of borders and praises his host nation, Boochani and Tofighian express their deep skepticism when they write how

> There is an island isolated in a silent ocean where people are held prisoner. The people cannot experience the world beyond the island ... They only see each other and hear the stories they tell one another ... they are frustrated by their isolation and incarceration, but they have also been taught to accept their predicament.
>
> News somehow enters the prison about another island where the mind is free to know and create ... The people on the other island ... see things that the prisoners cannot ... create things that the prisoners cannot ... know things that the prisoners cannot ... One island kills vision, creativity and knowledge—it imprisons thought. The other island fosters vision, creativity and knowledge—it is a land where the mind is free.
>
> The first island is the settler-colonial state called Australia, and the prisoners are the settlers.
>
> The second island contains Manus Prison, and knowledge resides there with the incarcerated refugees.[27]

After Boochani transmitted that knowledge via text messages from a smuggled, contraband phone, Tofighian assembled Boochani's book from these messages.[28] On the one hand, a hostage with a cell phone. On the other hand, the Australian nation-state, its prison apparatus and client states, its armed guards and lawyers, its ships and airplanes. An asymmetric conflict, waged by the refugee with words and symbols. As Boochani says: "I create my own discourse and do not succumb to the language of oppressive power. I create my own language."[29]

The nation-state upholds the language of realism, for against the brutal punishments of a prison island, the realistic response for the refugees should be submission and voluntary deportation. Boochani resists both deportation and realism, writing what his translator describes as "horrific surrealism."[30] I can think of no better term or genre to describe the voyage of the illegitimate, uninvited border crosser, blamed by countries and citizens for breaking laws and borders. Nation-states are essentially conservative, their autocratic violence enforcing borders along the nation's edge and within the nation as well, policing potentially unruly others. Many of these nations are responsible for creating conditions depriving millions of opportunities for life, forcing them to make a choice between heroism at home or heroism in exile. That difficult choice is the reason refugees and other border crossers become the avant garde for a world without borders—a world that can be nightmare or dream, hell or heaven.

I return to my father, his earthly journey nearly complete. He has already, in the words of Homer, sailed "over the wine-dark sea to men of strange speech."[31] In the epic that is his life, his epithet is the Father, mine the Son. I always thought of my father as a conservative man who enforced the borders of my life with lessons about Catholicism and capitalism, authority and respect, suffering and sacrifice. But in so many ways he has preceded me by making choices I never had to make, as when he fled his homeland, twice. Sometimes his choices showed me that I could make them too, as when I finally became a father. He will continue being my own personal vanguard, venturing before me once more across the final border to the ultimate exile, showing me, his son of strange speech, the inevitable way to our last continent.

5.   ON BEING MINOR

I am an American, not quite native-born, true, but mostly bred in this country, raised in Silicon Valley where the future always shines brightly, a fate in many ways major, which is to say it is a big deal, as all things American must be. But as major as my citizenship is, I am also a minority, or so my government classifies me through its census.

The connotations of being minor are often negative, or at least lesser: athletes in the minor leagues, an artist's minor works, a minority's minor feelings. To be minor is to be unimportant, casually dismissed, of lesser ability, easy to exploit, vulnerable to danger, in need of protection. Being minor might mean being smaller in number relative to a larger population, as when one is a minority, but sometimes a majority might have less power than a minority, as when small gangs of well-armed foreigners colonized large populations of natives. Patriarchy sometimes offers another example, as in the United States, which has slightly more women, at 50.4 percent, than men, but where women might still be considered minor, earning 82 cents to the dollar compared to men while comprising 85 percent of domestic violence victims.[1]

Being minor is partly about numbers and partly about power. Where they meet shapes our perception of who is minor and what that means. Even those comfortably in the majority, whether through size or power, may feel minor if their privileges become contested. The majority, however defined, strikes back partly out of fear that the minority seeks to replace them, doing essentially what the majority might have done to others in order to become major. This fear extends to culture as well, where symbolic war manifests in the struggle over whose stories are told and taught.

This sense of being a minority has been with me from some of my earliest memories in the United States, although I would not have called myself a minority, the word and idea too complicated for my childhood self. I would also not have called myself a minor, someone small, underage, not yet autonomous. Although I am now undeniably an adult, a sense of being a minor still persists despite being a father of two. So long as my own father lives, I am still his son, a feeling bordering on a kind of paralysis that descends on me the moment I return to his house, where I spent many childhood hours lying in bed, reading and fantasizing about becoming a writer. At the beginning of my literary dreams as a boy, I aspired to be major, even though I greatly enjoyed minor pleasures, from comic books to science fiction, fantasy, and mysteries. I knew these kinds of stories did not belong to the genre that refuses to call itself a genre, which reserves for itself the name of literature, so I set out to educate myself in my adolescence by reading Austen, Dickens, Thackeray, Dumas, Twain, Hardy, the Brontës, Hemingway, Fitzgerald, and Steinbeck, among many others who needed no first names. Reading everything from the minor to the major entertained and enlightened me, not just illuminating my mind but rendering me weightless, making me easy to transport, as if fired by a rocket, into distant worlds.

Along with my self-education came my formal education, which was Catholic and culminated in four years at a Jesuit all-boys college preparatory that sought to turn us into "Men for Others," as the Jesuit slogan went. This was the 1980s, when death squads murdered Jesuit priests and Catholic nuns in El Salvador. The assassins had trained at the School of the Americas in Fort Benning, Georgia, where my future father-in-law, as yet unbeknownst to me, had once completed his own airborne training in the segregated 1950s along with other South Vietnamese paratroopers. My future father-in-law and his comrades were being schooled to defend freedom and democracy, while some of the martyred clergy practiced liberation theology, the only Catholic doctrine that attracted me.

During my Jesuit years, I instinctively understood that art was liberating, just as religion was also supposed to free us from the world and our bodies. My school curriculum included the Bible, as major as it gets, along with many examples of the human word, like *The Sound and the Fury, Ulysses, The Communist Manifesto, The Bell Jar,* and *The Color Purple.* The authors of these works might be considered minor in some way: William Faulkner, a regional writer from the American South; James Joyce, an exile—who eventually went blind—from a colonized Ireland; Karl Marx and Friedrich Engels, waging intellectual guerilla war; Sylvia Plath, a white woman; Alice Walker, a Black queer woman. Each was so successful in making a major language their own that it might be difficult to hear the minor notes of their biographies, at least as they are taught in schools. But if I could cite Faulkner, Marx, and Joyce using only their surnames, thus acknowledging how they had ascended to the genre that does not call itself a genre, were Plath and Walker still examples of genres that are called genres—women's literature, Black literature, Black women's literature?

The minor itself is a genre, while the major is not, unless it is contested. The contrast between minor and major usually works to outline the minor, as when Zora Neale Hurston wrote, "I feel most colored when I am thrown against a sharp white background."[2] To foreground the major and name it as such, as in the case of whiteness or maleness or wealthiness, can discomfit those unused to being thrust into the foreground by the choice of others rather than by their own choosing. To label Faulkner, Marx, and Joyce not as individual geniuses but as examples of Dead White Male literature is to describe major Western literature as simply a genre versus a canon. The half-serious, half-mocking label of Dead White Male literature offends those who do not think something as noble and rarefied as literature should be demeaned by biological features. But the minor is always stigmatized in that fashion, which does not mean that the stigmas should be denied by those so marked.

By college, I understood the distinction between major and minor intuitively, and I had acquired the taste of an adolescent, alienated, angst-ridden white boy with artistic leanings, as confirmed by *Dead Poets Society,* which came out my freshman year. The movie featured a band of adolescent, alienated, angst-ridden white boys at an elite prep school and their inspiring literature teacher. When the boys quoted romantic poems to each other, I recognized the first one instantly, having memorized it years before—Shakespeare's Sonnet 18, "Shall I compare thee to a summer's day?" I then predicted the second poem the boys quoted to each other, which I had also memorized: Lord Byron's "She Walks in Beauty." Memorization was a form of mimicry, and I was already like a character from a V. S. Naipaul novel, one of those who "pretended to be real, to be learning, to be preparing ourselves for life, we mimic men of the New World."[3]

The part of me that wanted to be major willingly believed in the Great Names, the Great Works, the Great Books because I believed in the Great Words: Art, Civilization, Humanism, and the Canon, "the best which has been thought and said in the world," as Matthew Arnold put it in *Culture and Anarchy.*[4] And who doesn't want the best? If the religious canon was for the Saints and the cultural canon was for the Immortals, the minor was for the merely mortal, those who failed to attain the promise of eternal afterlife via religion or culture. At a young age, I aspired to immortality, even though I had no emotional understanding of death. But it was my intellectual understanding of death, born from studying the experiences of minoritized and colonized peoples, that introduced me to a different understanding of being minor than the one where the minor connoted failure or lack of importance or childhood, all characteristics that the majority has used to define, demean, and dominate a minority, as when Saul Bellow asked, "Who is the Tolstoy of the Zulus? The Proust of the Papuans?"[5] In contrast to that provocation—a Jewish American writer allying himself with the Western canon, thrown into relief against Africans and Pacific Islanders—being minor could also be a choice, a form of authorship in opposition to authority.

In this vein, the philosophers Gilles Deleuze and Félix Guattari wrote a book called *Kafka: Toward a Minor Literature,* which reclaimed Franz Kafka from his elevated status as one of the great twentieth-century writers and returned him to the same bed where Gregor Samsa opened his eyes to discover that he had become an insect. Kafka was a Jew writing in German in early twentieth-century Prague, and perhaps Samsa's metamorphosis into an insect foreshadowed the fate of European Jewry. Kafka's work could be read simply as universal literature, or also as minor literature tied to Kafka's historical, worldly situation, so that *Kafkaesque* could signify both individual and collective alienation and absurdity.

While Kafka is interesting as an artistic saint, he is also just as compelling as a writer who was mostly unknown when he died, as minor as John Keats, who asked that his epigraph be "Here lies one whose name was writ in water," or Emily Dickinson, who barely published in her lifetime. One of her poems is as relevant today as it was in nineteenth-century Massachusetts:

> I'm Nobody! Who are you?
> Are you—Nobody—too?
> Then there's a pair of us!
> Don't tell! They'd advertise—you know!
>
> How dreary—to be—Somebody!
> How public—like a Frog—
> To tell one's name—the livelong June—
> To an admiring Bog![6]

A poem about anonymity, written in anonymity, embodies the minor. But Kafka, Keats, and Dickinson are now major, and in contrast to them exist those many minor writers who have stayed minor. The scholar Louis Renza wrote a book about one of them, Sarah Orne Jewett, an American of the nineteenth and early twentieth century who influenced Willa Cather, was known to Henry James, and who authored nearly twenty books, the best-known being *The Country of the Pointed Firs*. While Jewett seems truly minor compared to Kafka, Keats, and Dickinson, her fate is not so terrible. A scholar devoted attention to her, and at least one of her books might still be read by a handful more than a century after her passing, which is more than can be said of most writers. How are we to judge who, among living or recently deceased writers, might one day become major? The library of my childhood was filled with thousands of books by writers I had never heard of, some quite famous in their time. And today, some dead authors whose names dominated only a decade or two ago are rarely mentioned, their life force no longer animating the "admiring bog" of the literary scene.

But literary reputation does not concern Deleuze and Guattari so much as the minor as a mode of opposition. For Deleuze and Guattari, the minor is always political. This does not predict the nature of those politics, or their possibilities and consequences. A classic example of such a disagreement over being minor and its relationship to politics and literature is found in James Baldwin's critique of what he called the "protest novel." Baldwin's examples are Harriet Beecher Stowe's *Uncle Tom's Cabin* and Richard Wright's *Native Son*. For Baldwin, while the protest novel "is an accepted and comforting aspect of the American scene," it is guilty of good intentions and bad writing.[7] *Uncle Tom's Cabin* might have been a massive nineteenth-century bestseller that promoted the antislavery cause, but it left behind the legacy of Uncle Tom himself as a figure of repugnant subservience and self-sacrifice.

Just as problematic, for Baldwin, is the protagonist of *Native Son*, Bigger Thomas, a poor young Black man from the Chicago ghetto who commits rape and murder. Baldwin writes that

Bigger is Uncle Tom's descendant . . . so exactly opposite a portrait that . . . it seems that the contemporary Negro novelist and the dead New England woman are locked in a deadly, timeless battle . . . black and white can only thrust and counter-thrust. . . . they go down into the pit together. . . . Bigger's tragedy is not that he is cold or black or hungry, not even that he is American, black; but that he has accepted a theology that denies him life, that he admits the possibility of his being sub-human and feels constrained, therefore, to battle for his humanity. . . . But our humanity is our burden, our life; we need not battle for it; we need only to do what is infinitely more difficult . . . accept it. The failure of the protest novel lies in its rejection of life, the human being, the denial of his beauty, dread, power, in its insistence that it is his categorization alone which is real and which cannot be transcended.[8]

I agree with much of what Baldwin says, and so, apparently, do many others, if we judge by a metric found in the author profiles of the *New York Times Book Review*. One standard question: "You're organizing a literary dinner party. Which three writers, dead or alive, do you invite?" This popularity contest is truly a trivial measure, but since human beings generally and writers specifically are vulnerable to pettiness, these invitations are a not-unworthy measure of where audiences place authors on the major to minor scale. The two authors with the most invitations to these soirees are William Shakespeare and James Baldwin, tied at thirty-two each. Emily Dickinson merited twelve, while Toni Morrison garnered eighteen invitations. Perhaps not surprisingly, she echoed Baldwin in advocating for what she calls "the human project—which is to remain human and to block the dehumanization and estrangement of others."[9]

Richard Wright does not seem to have ever been invited to one of these literary dinner parties (neither did poor Keats, but at least Kafka got the nod from Salman Rushdie).[10] Wright remains best known for Bigger Thomas, and the blunt, ferocious style of *Native Son,* which makes it unforgettable for me and discomfiting for some other readers. This violates what might be the first rule of a dinner party: do not make anyone uncomfortable. Those who are major can afford not to cause a fuss. They can be genteel, liberal, apolitical, because the politics of the normal, the normative, the standard, are the favored cause of the major—in other words, an invisible politics, one that does not have to acknowledge its political nature. The luxury and appearance of being apolitical comes at no cost for the powerful, whereas being apolitical for the minor reinforces a status quo that disadvantages them. Baldwin and Morrison are quite political, but they express their commitments with a literary gracefulness. This allows them to be both minor, as they unfailingly write about and center Black experiences, and also major, literally being given a seat at the table.

Although Baldwin and Morrison are correct about being unapologetic concerning one's humanity, Wright chose a different, less graceful approach with Bigger Thomas, who still deserves to be among the cast depicting Black and other human experiences—not the only character, just one of them. Wright mounts a vigorous explanation of his provocative aesthetic in *Native Son* through his essay "How 'Bigger' Was Born," including his belief that "Bigger Thomas was not black all the time; he was white, too, and there were literally millions of him, everywhere."[11] Baldwin disputed the prophetic power of *Native Son,* but Wright's explanation of why some Black Americans in 1940 were attracted by the spectacle of Japanese imperial might and by Hitler, Mussolini, and Stalin seems resonant today when Wright talks about the "wild and intense longing . . . to belong, to be identified, to feel that they were alive as other people were, to be caught up forgetfully and exultingly in the swing of events, to feel the clean, deep, organic satisfaction of doing a job in common with others."[12] This populist solidarity, enthralled with fascism, cruelty, and collective violence, is not something we have left behind; it exists as the shadow of expansive solidarity. While expansive solidarity calls for collective liberation, populist solidarity calls for selective liberation, carried out at the expense of demonized others.

Condemned to death but thinking he has freed himself in his own mind, Bigger Thomas embodies that limited vision of liberation. He unsettles some readers because he resists the sentimental impulse of literature, at least the kind of writing often praised by well-meaning readers, myself included at times, who seek to defend the value of literature in a debased age, which is probably every age, according to writers. This sentimentalism is the major urge to believe that literature is good for you, like vegetables or organic food, that it can improve us, elevate us, teach us empathy. But much of the impact of *Native Son* depends on its depiction of Bigger Thomas as someone who refuses to agree with the moralizing lure of redemption or the call for a shared humanity. Bigger says, "What I killed for must've been good! .... When a man kills, it's for something. . . . I didn't know I was really alive in this world until I felt things hard enough to kill for 'em. It's the truth."[13] While Baldwin decries the master-slave dialectic that condemns both white and Black to the abyss, it seems that Wright knows exactly what he is doing: showing that the abyss remains open at our feet.

Wright traces his creation of Bigger Thomas to the reaction to his first book, *Uncle Tom's Children,* a collection of novellas from 1936. "I had made an awfully naïve mistake . . . I had written a book which even bankers' daughters could read and weep over and feel good about. . . . if I ever wrote another book, no one would weep over it . . . it would be so hard and deep that they would have to face it without the consolation of tears."[14] Nothing is inherently wrong with tears or bankers' daughters, but Wright implies that emotionally appealing to women, who often constitute the majority of readers, is both the route to popularity and also something potentially demeaning to the writer. Ironically, the rage of *Native Son,* combined with Wright's artistry, led the book to become a critical and commercial success, sealing Wright's reputation as a major writer, if a troubling one.

While Baldwin criticized a protest novel such as *Native Son* for appealing to liberals, those same liberals now quote Baldwin's writing as literary scripture. But Baldwin can no more control his reception than

Wright can determine his, because as Black people in the United States, they shared, in Baldwin's words, a "lot . . . as ambiguous as a tableau by Kafka."[15] Ralph Ellison stresses a similar theme in his explanation about his literary strategy in *Invisible Man*: "the aim is a realism dilated to deal with the almost surreal state of our everyday American life."[16] This is why Deleuze and Guattari think of the minor as always politicized, for the minor is, by definition, dropped into a pit or an abyss not of their making. The Kafkaesque nature of racial alienation means that in the parable of Baldwin and Wright, neither offers a better solution than the other. Both of the routes with which they are identified, respectively emphasizing humanity or inhumanity, are insufficient in and of themselves and captured easily enough by the ministers of the canon, ready to dilute provocations with a generous sprinkle of holy water.

Baldwin and Wright were not only minor writers in terms of race in the United States. They were also minor writers within empires, the American and the French, and both moved to France and died there as exiles or even, perhaps, as refugees. Wright died in Paris in 1960 with the American empire still ascendant, not yet checked by the war in Việt Nam. Before his death, he had traveled through Africa, met with anticolonial leaders, and attended the Bandung Conference in Indonesia. Aware of the French war in Algeria, which killed over a million Algerians, and in which Algerian revolutionaries killed a fair number of the French, Wright kept silent for fear of offending his French hosts, given that he could not return to the United States. One way of understanding the difference between Wright as an author and Bigger Thomas as a character can be found in the work of Frantz Fanon, who died a year after Wright. Like Baldwin, Fanon in his early work recognized the necessity of claiming one's humanity without apology. At the end of *Black Skin, White Masks,* he wrote that "It is through the effort to recapture the self and to scrutinize the self, it is through the lasting tension of their freedom that men will be able to create the ideal conditions of existence for a human world."[17] Fanon also argues for the need "to touch the other, to feel the other, to explain the other to myself."[18] But while this might be possible for the individual purely through an act of will, Fanon would conclude that recognizing the other would not be enough for collective political freedom when the colonizer simply refuses to leave.

In *The Wretched of the Earth*—written after his service to the Algerian revolution—Fanon considered the necessity, even inevitability, of armed struggle against colonization, even if that violence inflicted terrible trauma on those who suffered it and those who wielded it, and even if that violence would not guarantee a just postcolonial society. The terrible violence of the Algerian revolution expressed what Wright captured in *Native Son,* which is why we need Wright as much as Baldwin, for that violence still persists. By the late 1960s, with the war in Việt Nam peaking, with Malcolm X, Medgar Evers, and Martin Luther King, Jr., assassinated, Baldwin was comparing the suppression of the Black Panthers to the American counterinsurgency against the Việt Cộng. If a younger Baldwin had decried what he considered to be the myth of an unreal Bigger Thomas, an older Baldwin endorsed the legend of the Black Panthers. The reality of the Black Panthers and the Việt Cộng was complicated, but in their most heroic mode, they threatened the unimpeded exercise of American violence domestically and internationally. By the time Baldwin died in France in 1987, however, the resurgence of the American empire, against what Ronald Reagan called the "Evil Empire" of the Soviet Union, was quite visible, although the United States is not so much an empire of territory, as in the British and French cases, but a constellation of military bases around the world.

An empire that does not call itself an empire, as it is with the United States, desires a literature that does not identify itself as a genre, but instead aspires to an invisible, unmarked universality, a majority that provides the background against which numerous minorities stand out, to be targeted or to be tokenized. I end with three poets who might one day be major but who I think are minor at the moment, by condition and possibly by choice. They grapple with the inevitability of violence that comes with being an empire's minor subjects. Their minor writing throws the empire into relief by appropriating the documents of American empire, subverting its language from inside.

In her book *Whereas,* Layli Long Soldier responds to President Barack Obama's 2009

> Congressional Resolution of Apology to Native Americans. No tribal
> leaders or official representatives were invited to witness and receive
> the Apology on behalf of tribal nations. . . .My response is directed to
> the Apology's delivery, as well as the language, crafting, and arrange-
> ment of the written document. I am a citizen of the United States and
> an enrolled member of the Oglala Sioux Tribe, meaning I am a cit-
> izen of the Oglala Lakota Nation—and in this dual citizenship, I must
> work, I must eat, I must art, I must mother, I must friend, I must listen,
> I must observe, constantly I must live.[19]

I am reminded of Deleuze and Guattari's argument that "the minor no longer designates specific literatures but the revolutionary conditions for every literature within the heart of what is called great (or estab-lished) literature."[20] They also ask:

> How many people today live in a language that is not their own? Or
> no longer, or not yet, even know their own and know poorly the major
> language they are forced to serve? This is the problem of immigrants,
> and especially of their children, the problem of minorities, the problem
> of a minor literature, but also a problem for all of us: how to tear a
> minor literature away from its own language, allowing it to challenge
> the language and making it follow a sober revolutionary path? How
> to become a nomad and an immigrant and a gypsy in relationship to
> one's own language?[21]

In a sense, Long Soldier answers Deleuze and Guattari with a series of poems that begin with "Whereas," that introductory word of the clauses that go into governmental documents, proclamations, and treaties, many of which the United States carried out with Native nations and then betrayed. The poet conjures the long-term consequences of genocide by attacking the bloodless legalese found in these "Whereas" clauses, as in this excerpt:

> WHEREAS I tire. Of my effort to match the effort of the statement: "Whereas Native Peoples and non-Native settlers engaged in numerous armed conflicts in which unfortunately, both took innocent lives, including those of women and children." I tire
>
> of engaging in numerous conflicts, tire of the word *both*. Both as a woman and a child of that Whereas. Both of words and wordplay, hunching over dictionaries. Tire of understanding weary, weakened, exhausted, reduced in strength from labor. Bored.[22]

Long Soldier reveals the symmetry in the government's "Whereas" clause to be a mendacious depiction of equal violence between settlers and Indigenous peoples. The seemingly neutral, reconciliatory language of both / and, which actually favors the colonizer, reminds me of President Jimmy Carter's statement in 1977 that "the destruction was mutual" between Americans and Vietnamese during the American war in Việt Nam.[23] This moral, material, and mortal equivalence is what Americans want to hear, even if it is patently, quantifiably false.

In another example, Long Soldier dwells on the language of Obama's apology, given that the words "apologize" or "sorry" do not exist in many Native languages:

> This doesn't mean that in Native communities where the word "apologize" is not spoken, there aren't definite actions for admitting and amending wrongdoing. Thus, I wonder how, without the word, this text translates as a gesture—

The United States, acting
Through Congress—
██████ on behalf of the
people of the United States to
all Native Peoples for the
many instances of violence,
maltreatment, and neglect
inflicted on Native Peoples
by citizens of the United
States;[24]

On the facing page, Long Soldier writes

I express commitment to reveal in a text the shape of its pounding—

followed by an array of words from the Congressional Resolution but
with spaces removed and syntax stripped. The words, forged into the
shape of a hammer, lose their meaning, exposing the emptiness of this
resolution and recalling, perhaps, the government language of earlier
generations that allowed the stealing of Native lands, the imprisonment
of Indigenous peoples on reservations, the kidnapping of their children.

Empires and war machines deploy the language of neutrality, bu-
reaucracy, and symmetry to disguise the impact of their asymmetrical
policies and weaponry. Stealth bombers require stealth language. The
poet Solmaz Sharif demonstrates this in *Look,* a book of poems ignited
by jargon drawn from the Dictionary of Military and Associated Terms
of the United States Department of Defense. She scatters these terms
throughout her book and responds to them, as in this poem:

CONTAMINATED REMAINS   wash hands before getting in bed
                        leave interrogation room before answering cell
                        teach your mouth to say
                        honey when you enter the kitchen

<pre>
DAMAGE AREA   does not include night sweats
                       or retching at the sight of barbeque

DEAD SPACE   fridges full
                       after the explosion the hospital
                       places body parts
                       out back where crowds
                       attempt to identify those
                       who do not answer their calls
                       by an eyeball
                       a sleeve of a favorite shirt
                       a stopped wristwatch

DESTRUCTION RADIUS   limited to blast site
                       and not the brother abroad
                       who answers his phone
                       then falls against the counter
                       or punches a cabinet door
</pre>

We turn to dictionaries to give us meaning, but the deadness of the military dictionary's language cloaks the deadly effects implied by the language. In contrast, the poet's minor language, versus the military dictionary's major language, shows us the human, empirical reality of empire. The language of the military dictionary is formally accurate, however, in expressing, through its sterility, the numbness of the average citizen of empire when it comes to the effects of that empire's power.

Another writer who responds via poetic form to the rationalizations of empire and its documents is Mai Der Vang. In her book *Yellow Rain,* she writes: "I am a daughter of Hmong refugees: mother and father were among the fled, which makes me among the fled."[25] Some of the Hmong fought alongside Americans during the war in Việt Nam, when the CIA and US Air Force waged the so-called "Secret War" in Laos. Tens of thousands of Hmong died, but the United States abandoned most of its

Hmong allies at war's end, and many Hmong became refugees. They recount being attacked by their enemies with a chemical weapon dropped from planes and helicopters, which they called "yellow rain." Those killed by yellow rain might have numbered six thousand, twenty thousand, or forty thousand.[26] Not trusting the Hmong as definitive sources on their own deaths, US officials investigated the incidents of yellow rain but could come to no conclusion as to whether yellow rain was or was not chemical warfare.

Against the imprecision of the death toll and the skepticism of Western scientists, Vang assembles a fearsome range of documents that she takes apart and reassembles, comments on, and mixes with her own poems: US embassy cables, maps, photos, historical facts, scientific studies, refugee questionnaires, and lab reports concerning the physical specimens of blood and urine taken from Hmong survivors, some of which "ARRIVED IN A DEPLORABLE CONDITION," according to a 1984 report.[27] A lab report the following year says "YOU MAY DESTROY THESE SAMPLES."[28] Vang also includes the testimonials of Hmong survivors, but since they are neither Western nor white, their evidence has not proven sufficient to Western and white authorities. The most notorious research was conducted by a Harvard scientist and his colleague at Yale, who decided that yellow rain was most likely bee feces. Vang writes: "They made the Hmong appear as if we were confused, as if we couldn't tell the difference between what the earth gave and what man made, the difference between shit and death."[29]

For Long Soldier, Sharif, and Vang, the major, official language they inhabit and subvert obfuscates through both precision and vagueness. The carefully worded apology, the efficient jargon, the scientific objectivity, all amount to symbolic weaponry, one that can be disassembled in a minor poetry that may not look like literature to some, given its incorporation of the nonliterary. (In case anyone might think being called minor is insulting, I also prefer to think of myself as minor, and some critics have even called me "ultraminor"—which might be too minor.)[30] The question is: why aspire to be major? For writers, being

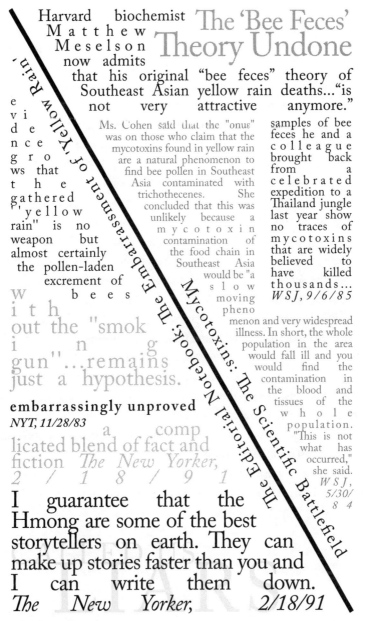

Harvard biochemist Matthew Meselson now admits

The 'Bee Feces' Theory Undone

that his original "bee feces" theory of Southeast Asian yellow rain deaths..."is not very attractive anymore."

evidence grows that the gathered 'yellow rain" is no weapon but almost certainly the pollen-laden excrement of bees

With out the "smoking gun"...remains just a hypothesis.

embarrassingly unproved
NYT, 11/28/83

a complicated blend of fact and fiction *The New Yorker, 2 / 1 8 / 9 1*

Ms. Cohen said that the "onus" was on those who claim that the mycotoxins found in yellow rain are a natural phenomenon to find bee pollen in Southeast Asia contaminated with trichothecenes. She concluded that this was unlikely because a mycotoxin contamination of the food chain in Southeast Asia would be "a slow moving phenomenon and very widespread illness. In short, the whole population in the area would fall ill and you would find the contamination in the blood and tissues of the whole population. "This is not what has occurred," she said. *WSJ, 5/30/84*

samples of bee feces he and a colleague brought back from a celebrated expedition to a Thailand jungle last year show no traces of mycotoxins that are widely believed to have killed thousands... *WSJ, 9/6/85*

Mycotoxins: The Scientific Battlefield

The Editorial Notebook: The Embarrassment of Yellow Rain.

I guarantee that the Hmong are some of the best storytellers on earth. They can make up stories faster than you and I can write them down. *The New Yorker, 2/18/91*

Mai Der Vang, excerpt from *Yellow Rain*. Copyright © 2021 by Mai Der Vang. Reprinted with permission of The Permissions Company, LLC on behalf of Graywolf Press.

consecrated as major might best be done when the author is dead (some writers would likely disagree), when the flesh of fame has decayed, leaving only the bones of the art. Consciously aspiring to be major as a living author could lead to major art, but it can also lead to collaboration with the ruling tastes of the day, shaped in my case by the politics of an empire that refuses to call itself an empire.

Empires can intoxicate themselves with the fumes of their power, while artists can likewise be seduced by the delusion of wanting to be major, as in the belief that one can master writing. Is such mastery possible, or is there always something in our art that eludes us? I think of my art as the calling that allows me to create and therefore approach something like the divine, which cannot be mastered. In a more earthly sense, while literature is sometimes still a major art form that can garner respect even in the most capitalist societies, literature is also minor in the popular sense, relative to the artistic and commercial juggernauts of movies and video games. Working in an art form that is major to me but minor to many others leaves me with a sense of humility before my calling, one that masters me more than I can master it.

I do admit to being human, however. Very human. I, too, like dinner party invitations, or at least the idea of them. Better invited than not invited, perhaps, but the thought of an afterlife spent attending an unending dinner party in a clean, well-lit room, surrounded by literary celebrities and the masters of the universe, congratulating each other on being the best and the brightest, occasionally gazing down with pity at the poor folks in the pit, fills me with dread. The underworld is warmer, and with the lights turned down low, perhaps a lot more fun.

6. ON THE JOY
OF OTHERNESS

N ow we come to an end, with so many things I have
not yet touched on when it comes to salvation and destruction, on writing as an other and writing about
otherness. Over the course of these lectures, I have aged, and with this
year, as with every passing year, I cannot help but hear the distant rumble
of "Time's wingèd chariot hurrying near."[1] My beloved, beautiful four-
year-old daughter heralded this chariot, not long ago. Over dinner, she
smiled at me with her eyes lit up, then leaned close and said, "Daddy,
you're old. You're going to die soon. I love you. Will there be a funeral?"

She probably will not remember these words. But I will, because
they touch on what I have kept for the end, the lightest and the heaviest
subject: the joy of otherness. This topic of joy is heavy, because I am a
pessimist. And when it comes to otherness, the associations are often
gloomy, revolving around victimization and marginalization or trauma
and erasure, all subjects in which I revel. But it is no wonder that some
who are othered would rather feel joy than pain. They simply yearn to
be human, although humanity itself comes with a heaviness inherent.

In the end, we cannot escape from otherness, because otherness exists within us and our humanity. Fernando Pessoa, who was born and

died in Lisbon, wrote that "To live is to be other," foreshadowing Derrida's concept of otherness as being elusive, and evoking, perhaps, the idea that otherness is more important as a principle and an orientation, rather than an identity, which can be self-serving.[2] Can we therefore find a degree of joy in our inevitable otherness, versus trying to do the impossible and dispel our otherness and our others, especially when doing so often involves shame and violence?

If that is a heavy subject to shoulder, Italo Calvino offers some guidance for how to bear that burden, at least for writers, although I think his lessons have wider meaning. In Calvino's Norton Lectures, *Six Memos for a New Millenium,* he examined the opposition between weight and lightness, and chose the latter: "When the human realm seems doomed to heaviness, I feel the need to fly like Perseus into some other space. I am not talking about escaping into dreams or into the irrational. I mean . . . the need . . . to look at the world from a different angle, with different logic, different methods of knowing and proving."[3] He challenges us to explore that human realm with a light touch, calling for "the sudden nimble leap of the poet / philosopher who lifts himself against the weight of the world, proving that its heaviness contains the secret of lightness, while what many believe to be the life force of the times—loud and aggressive, roaring and rumbling—belongs to the realm of death, like a graveyard of rusted automobiles."[4]

I have groped my way intuitively through this graveyard as I attempted to become a writer, grappling with Very Serious Subjects and Very Important Literature. Otherness was a major concern, but it was the alterity of sociological, political, historical categories: race, class, gender, nationality, and so on. What I had not grappled with was the otherness of those who had been right next to me from my origins, my mother and father, my older brother, my oldest sister, whom we had left behind in Việt Nam at the end of war, where, in the aftermath, the victors dispatched her to labor on a youth brigade to rebuild the country, a fate that could have been mine.

Perhaps partly because of this fear of understanding my siblings and my own parents, I had no desire to be a parent, to test myself with children and my own family as my parents had been tested by me and my siblings. Writing was the only creative act that interested me, not fathering, and so when I learned that my first child was due to arrive—I panicked. My life, as I knew it, was over, and it hardly seemed fair, for I had not yet finished my novel. But my son's impending birth focused me, and I completed the draft a few days before his birth. For the next few months, I revised the novel at night while this strange new being slept, so small and light, yet so heavy on my conscience and my soul.

He lay swaddled and immobilized on the futon in his mother's office while I sat at her desk, keeping an eye on Little Oedipus as I wrestled with sentences, word choices, rhythms. Anytime my heir stirred, which was often, I stuck a bottle of formula in his mouth, a story over which he now chortles. I rewrote and kept vigil until three in the morning. Then it was my turn to sip on my formula—single malt Scotch—until five in the morning, when his mother took over. So it was that we fattened our son and kept him alive.

My infant son was my other, perhaps still is an other to me in a wondrous way, as I must be some looming other to my daughter, intimate and yet incomprehensible. I think I know my son very well, but perhaps I do not know him at all. And why would I want to know him, or my daughter, completely? It is impossible that they would know me absolutely. The reserve of our own mystery to ourselves and to our closest others is a source of consternation, but also, potentially, joy.

Becoming a father frightened me more than anything, including writing, which caused me much anguish that I willingly embraced. Writing, like God, is an incomprehensible other that can inspire as much as torment. Writing requires faith as well as a willingness to abide mystery, the unknown source from where creativity emerges. Still, much of creativity springs not from magic or mystique but from dull discipline, as in Haruki Murakami's idea that writing is mostly a matter of routine, even punishment, until it is not. In his memoir *What I Talk About When I Talk About Running,* Murakami compares writing to running, particularly marathons, including the original marathon route in Greece, and even running an ultramarathon of sixty-two miles. I run a few miles on a treadmill in my basement next to the washing machine and dryer, watching instructors on my phone exhort me to reach my goal with clichés so trite I would be appalled to write them. Nevertheless, the exhortations work, encouraging me to run a few more miles, which inspires me to think I can write a few more pages.

Perhaps Murakami's novels themselves express that relationship between the mundane and the mysterious, his narrators rather unremarkable, even his prose somewhat flat, all contrasted against a moment when the surreal or the weird disrupts the routine and reveals a parallel world that might swallow up a character. In his novel *Sputnik Sweetheart,* for example, a woman on vacation finds herself stuck on a Ferris wheel. She can see her apartment, and using binoculars to look into her room, sees herself or someone exactly like her having sex with an unknown man. This external shock of an inexplicable world bifurcates her internally and leads to a sense of losing another self that she has just discovered.

Oneself as another, oneself as the other—perhaps one reason for my fascination with these manifestations of otherness is because of how much the creative process seems to be a relationship both to the puzzling, occasionally sublime world outside of ourselves and the haunting otherness inside ourselves. The primal scene of witnessing one's own otherness can be traumatic, with the treatment of our others being sometimes vicious and violent, exploitative and murderous. But willfully accessing one's otherness through something like a creative act possesses elements of joy, at least for me, even if that access can usually only be found through hard work, tedious routine, and a degree of pain. I acknowledge the pain, even if I resist romanticizing it, for the fetishized suffering of the individual male artist is not deserving of more attention than the pain of manual labor or of actual childbirth, which canonical art has usually treated as a minor theme.

The grand cliché of tortured artists struggling with the mystery of creation, of their own otherness, could be deflated by the possibility that writing on average is less painful, dramatic, and life-risking than laboring, whether that means toiling in fields or mines or enduring pregnancy and childbirth. A series of small clichés composes the romantic idea of the genius artist: the procrastination, the self-flagellation, the periodic reminders from agents and editors that writing is as much business as art, the constant inflation and deflation of the ego as writers veer between delusions of grandeur and paroxysms of despair. These clichés accumulate in their banality, but it is the pedestrian nature of writing—one step after the next, over and over—that allows access to those fleeting moments of joy found in the otherness of creation.

Reflecting on my parents, whose devotion to capitalism and Catholicism I rebelled against, I can see now, with the forgiving distance of time, far removed from the dim recesses of the SàiGòn Mới, that they were creative people. Entrepreneurs. Are founders of small businesses any less inspired than writers who publish in small magazines? The reverse is also true, that the contributions of such writers, their ability to access the joy of otherness through writing, is no less important than what capitalists accomplish. The creativity of my parents enabled my inventive urges, and their hard, arduous labor, grounded in the unglamorous and dangerous reality of a grocery store where they stood all day, made it possible for me to sit in a chair, gaze at a screen, and fiddle with my word count in between doses of social media.

The act of creativity, whether that of my parents or me, is carried out in the face of vast indifference. The monk Thích Nhất Hạnh, in *Fragrant Palm Leaves,* expressed something similar when he stood before the Vietnamese landscape: "The forest was so immense, we felt minuscule. I think we shouted to overcome our feeling of being utterly insignificant."[5] Shouting into the wilderness is what the act of creation can feel like, our human voices measured against the vast powers of the natural and mystical worlds. Even a fabled spiritual leader like Thích Nhất Hạnh needed to shout sometimes, not as an aberration from spiritual discipline but perhaps the periodic expression of it, as the occasional book from a writer expresses years of quiet and self-controlled labor.

I imagine a parallel exists between creative and religious discipline. The religious rely on the daily drills of rituals, texts, and prayers to remind themselves that God exists, with God and the divine being our human way of trying to understand the ultimate act of creation—how we and our world came into being. My parents prayed every day, and although I do not believe in their God, I am moved by the fact that when my mother died, she could still, despite her diminishment, recite the Lord's Prayer with my father. Contemplating her passage into some other realm, I take comfort in Thích Nhất Hạnh's words about his own mother's death: "For the first four years after she died, I felt like an orphan. Then one night she came to me in a dream, and from that moment on, I no longer felt her death as a loss."[6] My mother has visited my brother in a dream, bringing him comfort, but she has never come to me, another mystery I do not understand.

Thích Nhất Hạnh continues about his mother: "I understood that she had never died, that my sorrow was based on illusion . . . She did not exist because of birth, nor cease to exist because of death. I saw that being and nonbeing are not separate. Being can exist only in relation to nonbeing, and nonbeing can exist only in relation to being. Nothing can cease to be."[7] I do not remember if I had read Thích Nhất Hạnh's words before I wrote my first novel. But the conclusion of *The Sympathizer* also concerns nothing, when the narrator reflects on the famous slogan of Hồ Chí Minh: "Nothing is more precious than independence and freedom." Those words helped motivate a revolution that freed Việt Nam from foreign interference and unified a country, as well as forcing my parents to flee. Nearly thirty years later, I returned to a Sài Gòn of the early 2000s still struggling with economic inequality and some disillusionment with the promises of communism, where I heard a sarcastic, possibly bitter joke that I would then include in the novel's conclusion: "What is more precious than independence and freedom? Nothing."

Some readers interpreted the ending as nihilistic, but that is not correct. To take inspiration from Thích Nhất Hạnh, nothing only exists in relation to something, and vice versa. God is only one of the most obvious examples of a nothing that one portion of humanity has turned into something, an otherness that elicits sacrifice and murder, joy and suffering, love and hate. Unlike me, who saw nothing when it came to God, my mother and father could see something. And my father, now having forgotten almost everything, can still say the Lord's Prayer. All one has to do is prompt him, and from somewhere deep inside the words emerge, unforgotten because of his life of discipline. I find it joyful to know that a deep well of otherness exists inside of him that I cannot detect, one that gives him life and hope.

I admire my father's discipline, the relentlessness of it that delivers a believer to the final destination, which is a confrontation with one's own otherness, carried out utterly in private and with that greater otherness that God symbolizes. I underestimated my father in some ways, as I grew in height and vanity until I was taller than he was, more fluent in English, more capable in the ways of the West and the canon of its high culture. And he was aware of my underestimation of him, as perhaps many parents know of their children's misjudgment of them.

Once my father and I found ourselves sitting in my car running an errand, and he suddenly said to me, "Remember that time we went to France and you told the French border officer that I did not speak English?" That trip had happened a decade before, but my father had obviously waited for his opportunity to let me know he had held on to the slight. He then picked up a book I had with me, *Lost in the City,* a collection of short stories by Edward P. Jones, who would later win the Pulitzer Prize for his novel *The Known World.* His short stories had moved me deeply and helped shape my own short story collection. My father read the opening paragraph of the first story, "The Girl Who Raised Pigeons," one of my favorite short stories, and translated it for me.

The story is about Betsy Ann, the girl of the title, and her single father, Robert, who live together in Washington, DC, the setting for all the stories of *Lost in the City*. Jones paints a portrait of an intimate Black neighborhood of 1957, "in those days, before the community was obliterated" by the construction of a railroad over the next four years.[8] Betsy Ann's mother has died in childbirth. The doctors "cut open her stomach and pulled out the child only moments after Clara died, mother and daughter passing each other as if along a corridor, one into death, the other into life."[9] A lonely child, Betsy Ann turns to raising pigeons as an act of love and mothering. The family friend who gives her the first pigeons calls them his "babies," with him as their "daddy."[10] Betsy Ann's relationship to her pigeons is likewise maternal, and "the idea of being on the roof with birds who wanted to fly away to be with someone else pained her."[11] Robert tries to protect Betsy Ann from the further mortal perils of life by checking the pigeon coop for dead pigeons before she wakes up each morning, but in the end, neither can protect the pigeons from an attack by rats that kills most of them. When the last of the surviving pigeons flies away at the end of the story, "She did nothing, aside from following him, with her eyes, with her heart, as far as she could."[12] The ending is poignant but perhaps carries a hint of joy, for flying away is as normal as can be, a move of life and independence that should be celebrated even as the break causes pain. When I graduated from high school and left for college, I was only joyful. I never looked back, perhaps fearful of being drawn back into my parents' world, and I gave not a thought to what my mother and father might have felt. I only cared that I was at last free, unburdened, escaping from a house of claustrophobic love.

"The Girl Who Raised Pigeons" explores the same territory of family cleaving, where cleaving brings people together and cleaving also splits them apart. The story is clearly about the natural cycle of birth and death, of parenting and letting go, drawing parallels between Robert's love for Betsy Ann and her love for her pigeons. While the killing of the pigeons and the death of Betsy Ann's mother are tragic, they are also part of this natural cycle. The railroad's destruction of the Black community, however, is not natural but is an outcome of a racial order that marginalizes and devalues Black life and love. Even in foregrounding the creeping sense of otherness between Robert and Betsy Ann, who gradually pulls away from her father as she grows up, Edward P. Jones is careful to show how the larger forces of otherness that have damaged and shaped Black life continue in their malevolence.

He does so with a light touch, despite the gravity of how white-dominated urban policy has shattered Black communities in many American cities. That light touch is also evident in the opening passage that my father pointed to as we sat in the car, slightly tense in our father-son relationship: Betsy Ann's "father would say years later that she had dreamed that part of it, that she had never gone out through the kitchen window at two or three in the morning to visit the birds. By that time in his life he would have so many notions about himself set in concrete. And having always believed that he slept lightly, he would not want to think that a girl of nine or ten could walk by him at such an hour in the night without his waking and asking of the dark, Who is it? What's the matter?"[13]

Betsy Ann is my son's age now. At nine or ten, she learned to tiptoe past her protective father, as my son may yet learn to deceive me, as I myself snuck out of my parents' home as a teenager while they slept, all of us pigeons yearning to fly the coop, buoyant and weightless, at least until death. "The Girl Who Raised Pigeons" moved me through the way it evokes the intimacy of the relationship between parent and child, the father's tenderness and the way it was unspoken, which reminds me very much of the way my parents interacted with me. There is estrangement in the father and daughter's apartment, however, the sense that they each have parts of themselves that the other will never know. That sense of otherness between loved ones may be infused with sadness and melancholy, but perhaps also some joy at the possibility of discovering ever additional layers within others and oneself, until at last one reaches a truth about oneself.

For me, that search has unfolded through two forms of creativity. One form is as a father who reproduced himself in his children, an act both unsurprising and always surprising. I do not mean to be sentimental about this reproduction. Everybody has been a child, but not everybody should be a parent. Not everyone is equipped to deal with the otherness of children, and I may yet fail, a prospect that worries me as much as the possibility of my own potential failure as a writer. The other form of creation that has compelled me to look within myself is writing. As Edwidge Danticat has put it, reflecting on her art as a writer, "I exploit no one more than myself."[14] Self-exploitation, self-exploration—both are crucial to the act of writing, which I think always involves a confrontation with one's self, even if one writes about others.

Jorge Luis Borges, in his Norton Lectures, *This Craft of Verse,* had this to say: "I have toyed with an idea—the idea that although a man's life is compounded of thousands and thousands of moments and days, those many instants and those many days may be reduced to a single one: the moment when a man knows who he is, when he sees himself face to face."[15] I do not know if Borges ever found himself face to face with himself, and I do not know if I have seen my genuine, authentic face either, even though I have looked at myself often, in the mirror and in my writing. Suspicious of authenticity—having been accused of being inauthentic many times—I suspect that in the end what my writing will uncover about my self, or my many selves, is that I am authentic only to my own inauthenticity.

The poet Theodore Roethke put his relationship of author to self another way in one of his poems, where he wrote:

> Being myself, I sing
> The soul's immediate joy.[16]

In my case, that is the joy of otherness, an awareness that even seeing oneself face to face means that the very notion of otherness is present. One can only come face to face with oneself if one is already at least twofold, encountering oneself in an actual mirror or in the mirror of one's soul. And what if, to complicate Borges, one sees that one has many faces rather than just two?

Fernando Pessoa, as person and artist, was someone who dwelled constantly on his own multiplicity. He is famous for creating many authorial selves and names through which he wrote, each one with its own distinctive character. In his best-known work translated into English, *The Book of Disquiet*, he wrote that "Each of us is more than one person, many people, a proliferation of our one self. . . . like a diverse but compact multitude, this whole world of mine, composed as it is of different people, projects but a single shadow, that of this calm figure who writes, leaning against Borges's high desk where I have come to find the blotter he borrowed from me."[17]

Whereas Roethke sang the soul's joy, Pessoa, working the same metaphor, hears his soul: "My soul is a hidden orchestra; I know not what instruments, what fiddlestrings and harps, drums and tambours I sound and clash inside myself. All I hear is the symphony."[18] Roethke presumably had to hear or feel his soul's joy before he could sing it, but he deployed the idea of a singular soul, whereas Pessoa describes his soul as a collective of musicians and instruments, paralleling his idea that the many selves inside of him lead to only one shadow. Our shadows are a part of us and not a part of us at the same time, which Pessoa recognizes when he says that "Seeing myself frees me from myself. I almost smile, not because I understand myself, but because, having become other, I'm no longer able to understand myself."[19]

Disquieting, indeed, to see the incomprehensible otherness within oneself, but also possibly joyful, to realize that one's own selves are an immense, possibly endless nation. Coming face to face with that imagined community of one's own self might be like the moment where Thích Nhất Hạnh finds himself before the vast forest and can only shout in response. For me, writing is my way of quieting, for a while, that paradoxical disturbance of being aware of my simultaneous multiplicity and insignificance. When I have not written for some stretch of time,

I become an irritable, unpleasant person—disquieted. Writing is my discipline, my calling, my form of secular prayer that quiets me. I agree with what the writer Maryse Condé once wrote about writing, that it "has given me enormous joy. I would rather compare it to a compulsion, somewhat scary, whose cause I have never been able to unravel."[20]

The otherness of the blank page elicits joy from the writer, even if the path to that joy can be arduous, even if that joy is fleeting and must be renewed with repeated confrontations with that blankness. The white page looms like an enigmatic face staring back at me, the face of an other that can elicit both terror and empathy, both murder and love, to paraphrase the philosopher Emmanuel Levinas.[21] The confrontation with the other is not easy, should not be easy, but perhaps one thing that writing teaches me about myself is that if we ultimately could look with joy on our others, rather than with fear, anger, and hatred, then we could create something new: stories and societies that are both about the needs of individuals and collectives, leading to a sense of our own singular shadow as being cast from many, simultaneous selves. "Either I'm nobody, or I'm a nation," Derek Walcott wrote, although from his opposition we could extrapolate a contrasting conclusion, that a nation is composed of nobodies who must nevertheless be acknowledged.[22]

Ralph Ellison hinted at this possibility of transforming the self, in his case through writing. He said that "the trick here is that of creating one's identity through the medium of one's chosen art."[23] Ellison was thinking of the challenges facing not only writers but Black writers, for whom identity cannot only be a matter of the singular self but always has some relationship to a Black world that is both joyfully chosen by many Black people and painfully imposed on them by white people and others. The poet Richard Wilbur articulates something similarly paradoxical when it comes to identity and writing, if the identity is that of being a writer. For Wilbur, "When a poet is being a poet . . . he cannot be concerned with anything but the making of a poem. . . . psychologically speaking, the end of writing is the poem itself. . . . To quote Robert Frost again, 'You do more good by doing well than by doing good.'"[24]

I agree, but where is the world in all of this, the world outside of the poem and the poet as much as the world inside the poem and the poet? Wilbur anticipates and responds when he says,

> and yet, of course, poetry is a deeply social thing—radically and incorrigibly social.... Writing poetry is talking to oneself. Yet it is a mode of talking to oneself in which the self disappears; and the product is something that, though it may not be *for* everybody, is *about* everybody. Writing poetry, then, is an unsocial way of manufacturing a thoroughly social product. Because he must shield his poetry in its creation, the poet, more than other writers, will write without recognition.... he is likely to look on honors and distinctions with the feigned indifference of a wallflower. Certainly he is pleased when recognition comes; for what better proof is there that for some people poetry is still a useful and necessary thing... like a shoe.[25]

I love this image of the poem as a shoe, the poem as both art and craft, inspiration and labor, useless and useful, the earthly sole that cannot avoid being grounded and trod on, and the spiritual soul that remains ever mysterious to us and to others. This is not a binary, this is a fusion, a pun, a play on words between the sole and the soul, with poetry and writing at their best when they play with words, a very serious matter requiring a light touch. Shoes are serious matters, as are poems, both requiring their makers to work with delicacy and discipline. Shoes are themselves light, but carry the weight of our entire bodies. Imagine poems as the shoes that the writer has cobbled together. Anyone can fit in those shoes.

But in order for you to stand in those shoes, they must be empty. Full of nothing. When my own novels touch on the subject of nothing, some readers are disturbed. They do not understand that nothing is sacred. To say that nothing is sacred is sacrilegious, and it also means at the same time that we should revere nothing, from the vast empty expanses of the universe to the void within ourselves. From this paradox and contradiction in which nothing is in fact *something,* I find the unsettling, perplexing, tragicomic joy of otherness, ranging from my own individual, weird, idiosyncratic, unique otherness to the collective, systemic otherness projected onto me and my kind, whatever my absurd, negated kind is. Among my kind is the Vietnamese, the Asian, the minoritized, the racialized, the colonized, the hybrid, the hyphenated, the refugee, the displaced, the artist, the writer, the smart ass, the bastard, the sympathizer, and the committed—all those out of step, out of tune, out of focus, even to themselves.

I recall those lines from *Macbeth* that you all know: "Life's but a walking shadow . . . / It is a tale / Told by an idiot, full of sound and fury / Signifying nothing."[26] I am the idiot you have put up with for so many hours, and the joke is on you. But of course the joke is mostly on me and my kind, which is the best and the worst kind of joke, the trick that life and death play on us. I think about the fact that my sister came to visit the United States for the first time as I finished writing this last lecture. As I drove her to tourist sights around southern California, she told me a story I had never heard before, which involved my maternal aunts coming to our home after my mother had fled from the communist invasion with my brother and me, leaving my sister behind to guard the property. The aunts took from the house what they wanted, including the gold that my mother had left behind for them to share with her daughter. The aunts did not share the gold, but they did share a secret. "Do you know why you were left behind?" they asked my sister. "Because you were adopted." This is how my sister discovered what my parents had never told her, that she had been an orphan.

At the moment of our abandoning her fifty years ago, amid the terror, chaos, and confusion of the end of the war, she had been a teenager who went by the name of Tuyết. The last and only time I had seen her since then was twenty years ago on my return to Việt Nam, where she by then was middle-aged and using the name of Hương. The next time I saw her in person, picking her up from the airport in Los Angeles, she had become a senior citizen and a grandmother. When my brother came to my house to visit her, it was the first they had seen each other in five decades. Almost our entire lives as siblings since the end of the war had passed as two or three flashes in time.

If this meeting after so many years was a bad joke, played on us by history, then hopefully it was softened a little by what had happened the night before my brother's visit. I wanted to be a good brother and had taken my sister to a private party for the cast and producers of a television show based on *The Sympathizer*. The party took place at a legendary hotel on Sunset Boulevard in Los Angeles, where rock stars and movie stars were rumored to have done scandalous things. My sister and I were the first to arrive. One of the most famous movie stars in the world arrived next. I snapped a picture of my sister with the movie star, and then the movie star had his photographer take portraits of my sister and me. "This happens all the time in Hollywood," I said to her. A good joke, I hope.

I end with the rest of Roethke's poem, which goes like this:

> What time's my heart? I care.
> I cherish what I have
> Had of the temporal:
> I am no longer young
> But the winds and waters are;
> What falls away will fall;
> All things bring me to love.[27]

Love was what brought my sister to the United States, to see her brothers but most especially, I think, our father. After Los Angeles, my sister flew to San José to visit him, whom she had not seen since his last visit to Việt Nam thirty years before. Our father spends his days in quiet contemplation, and when I return, he either does not recognize me or pretends to recognize me, his other, as he is other to me. I warned my sister that our father would probably not know who she was, but this did not appear to deter her. When she walked into his room, she told me later, she asked him if he recognized her. In a moment of reunion and recognition that I think of as manifesting the joy of otherness, he murmured an assent. Then our father said, "*Vui lắm.*" And my sister was content that our father said he was very happy.

Notes

Bibliography

Acknowledgments

Index

NOTES

1. ON THE DOUBLE, OR INAUTHENTICITY

1. Giorgio Agamben, *Homo Sacer: Sovereign Power and Bare Life,* trans. Daniel Heller-Roazen (Redwood, CA: Stanford University Press, 1998).
2. Edward W. Said, *Reflections on Exile and Other Essays* (Cambridge, MA: Harvard University Press, 2002), 181.
3. Pierre Bourdieu, *The Field of Cultural Production* (New York: Columbia University Press, 1993), 75.
4. Czeslaw Milosz, *The Witness of Poetry* (Cambridge, MA: Harvard University Press, 1983), 18–19.
5. Toni Morrison, *The Origin of Others* (Cambridge, MA: Harvard University Press, 2017).
6. Anthony Veasna So, *Afterparties* (New York: Harper Collins, 2021), 16.
7. So, *Afterparties,* 62.
8. Bao Phi, *Sông I Sing* (Minneapolis: Coffee House Press, 2011), 38–39.
9. William Shakespeare, *The Complete Works of Shakespeare,* ed. W. J. Craig (London: Humphrey Milford, Oxford University Press, 1924), I.ii.363–364.
10. Chinua Achebe, *Home and Exile* (New York: Penguin Random House, 2001), 33. *Mister Johnson* by Joyce Cary was originally published in 1939 under the title *Power in Men.*
11. Achebe, *Home and Exile,* 29.
12. Arthur Rimbaud, letter to Paul Demeny, Charleville, May 15, 1871, in *Correspondance inédite (1870–1875) d'Arthur Rimbaud,* ed. Roger Gilbert-Lecomte (Paris: Éditions des cahiers libres, 1929), 51–63.
13. Evelyn Nien-Ming Ch'ien, *Weird English* (Cambridge, MA: Harvard University Press, 2005).
14. So, *Afterparties,* 178.
15. So, *Afterparties,* 194.
16. So, *Afterparties,* 185.
17. Herman Melville, *Moby-Dick* (Boston: Houghton Mifflin, 1955), 332.

2. ON SPEAKING FOR AN OTHER

1. Viet Thanh Nguyen, "War Years," in *The Refugees* (New York: Grove Press, 2017), 72.
2. William Carlos Williams, *In the American Grain* (New York: Albert and Charles Boni, 1925), 41.

3. Wikipedia, s.v. "Trần Văn Dĩnh," accessed March 10, 2024, https://en.wikipedia.org/wiki/Trần _Văn_Dĩnh.

4. Viet Thanh Nguyen, *Nothing Ever Dies: Vietnam and the Memory of War* (Cambridge, MA: Harvard University Press, 2017), 1.

5. E-mail to my agent, Nat Sobel: December 3, 2013. The editor shall remain unnamed.

6. Arundhati Roy, "Peace & the New Corporate Liberation Theology," City of Sydney Peace Prize Lecture, Sydney, Australia, November 3, 2004.

7. Maxine Hong Kingston, *The Woman Warrior* (New York: Alfred A. Knopf, 1976), 3.

3. ON PALESTINE AND ASIA

1. Isaac Chotiner, "The Brutal Conditions Facing Palestinian Prisoners," *New Yorker,* March 21, 2024; Osama Abu Rabee, "Palestinian Detainees Say They Faced Abuse in Israeli Jails," *Reuters,* June 12, 2024.

2. Jan Carew, "Going Beyond the Clichés," *New York Times,* September 22, 1974.

3. Shawn Wong, Facebook message to author, November 15, 2023.

4. Jeffery Paul Chan, "The Chinese in Haifa," in *Aiiieeeee! An Anthology of Asian-American Writers* (Washington, DC: Howard University Press, 1974), 77.

5. Chan, "The Chinese in Haifa," 90.

6. Chan, "The Chinese in Haifa," 92.

7. Joseph Conrad, *Heart of Darkness* (Cambridge: Cambridge University Press, 2018), 7.

8. Julie Otsuka, *The Buddha in the Attic* (New York: Knopf, 2011), 25.

9. Mahmoud Darwish, *Memory for Forgetfulness: August, Beirut, 1982* (Berkeley: University of California Press, 1995), 159.

10. Darwish, *Memory for Forgetfulness,* 32.

11. Darwish, *Memory for Forgetfulness,* 172.

12. Darwish, *Memory for Forgetfulness,* 179.

13. Darwish, *Memory for Forgetfulness,* 180.

14. Darwish, *Memory for Forgetfulness,* 181.

15. Darwish, *Memory for Forgetfulness,* 182.

16. Nadine Gordimer, *Writing and Being* (Cambridge, MA: Harvard University Press, 1995), 94.

17. Gordimer, *Writing and Being,* 104.

18. Gordimer, *Writing and Being,* 106.

19. Gordimer, *Writing and Being,* 108.

4. ON CROSSING BORDERS

1. Amitava Kumar, *Bombay—London—New York* (London: Routledge, 2002, repr., 2012), 226.

2. Jhumpa Lahiri, "The Third and Final Continent," in *Interpreter of Maladies* (Boston: Houghton Mifflin, 1999), 198.

3. Ha Jin, preface to *The Writer as Migrant* (Chicago: University of Chicago Press, 2008), x.

4. Ken Chen, "I Was Ostensibly Searching for My Father, But.," Poetry Foundation, April 14, 2016, https://www.poetryfoundation.org/harriet-books/2016/04/i-was-ostensibly-searching-for-my -father-but.

5. Viet Thanh Nguyen, *The Sympathizer* (New York: Grove Press, 2015), 192.

6. Gloria Anzaldúa, *Borderlands / La Frontera: The New Mestiza* (San Francisco: Aunt Lute Books, 1987), from the unpaginated preface.

7. Anzaldúa, *Borderlands / La Frontera,* 2–3.

8. Anzaldúa, *Borderlands / La Frontera,* 3.

9. Anzaldúa, *Borderlands / La Frontera*, 3.
10. Theresa Cha, *Dictee* (Berkeley: University of California Press, 2001), 75.
11. Cha, *Dictee*, 20.
12. Cha, *Dictee*, 56.
13. Cha, *Dictee*, 32.
14. Cha, *Dictee*, 141.
15. Behrouz Boochani, *No Friend But the Mountains: Writing from Manus Prison*, trans. Omid Tofighian (London: Picador Australia, 2018), 257.
16. Boochani, *No Friend But the Mountains*, 70.
17. Boochani, *No Friend But the Mountains*, 72.
18. Boochani, *No Friend But the Mountains*, 82–83.
19. Boochani, *No Friend But the Mountains*, "prison," 121, "zoo," 122, "degrade," 83–84.
20. Boochani, *No Friend But the Mountains*, 209, "half dead," Anzaldúa, *Borderlands / La Frontera*, 87.
21. Boochani, *No Friend But the Mountains*, 141.
22. Boochani, *No Friend But the Mountains*, "soldiers," "prisoners," 329, "subjects," 124.
23. Boochani, *No Friend But the Mountains*, 107.
24. Boochani, *No Friend But the Mountains*, 98–99.
25. Boochani, *No Friend But the Mountains*, 358.
26. Boochani, *No Friend But the Mountains*, 358.
27. Boochani, *No Friend But the Mountains*, 359–360.
28. Boochani, *No Friend But the Mountains*, 358.
29. Boochani, *No Friend But the Mountains*, 369.
30. Boochani, *No Friend But the Mountains*, 366.
31. Homer, *The Odyssey*, trans. A. T. Murray, rev. George E. Dimock (Cambridge, MA: Harvard University Press, 1919), 178.

5. ON BEING MINOR

1. US Census, 2021; Carolina Aragão, "Gender Pay Gap in the US Hasn't Changed Much in Two Decades," Pew Research Center, March 1, 2023, https://www.pewresearch.org/short-reads/2023/03/01/gender-pay-gap-facts/; Shannan Catalano, "Intimate Partner Violence, 1993–2010," Special Report, US Department of Justice, Bureau of Justice Statistics, November 2012, rev. September 29, 2015, 3, https://bjs.ojp.gov/content/pub/pdf/ipv9310.pdf.
2. Zora Neale Hurston, *How It Feels to Be Colored Me* (New York: Open Road Media, 2024), 3.
3. V. S. Naipaul, *The Mimic Men* (London: Penguin Books, 1967), 146.
4. Matthew Arnold, *Culture and Anarchy: An Essay in Political and Social Criticism* (London: Smith, Elder, and Co., 1889), viii.
5. James Atlas, "Chicago's Grumpy Guru," *New York Times Magazine*, January 3, 1988.
6. Emily Dickinson, "I'm Nobody! Who Are You?" in *The Poems of Emily Dickinson, Volume 1*, ed. R. W. Franklin (Cambridge, MA: Belknap Press of Harvard University Press, 1998), 279.
7. James Baldwin, *Notes of a Native Son* (Boston: Beacon Press, 1955), 19.
8. James Baldwin, *Notes of a Native Son* (Boston: Beacon Press, 1955), 22–23.
9. Toni Morrison, *The Origin of Others* (Cambridge, MA: Harvard University Press, 2017), 36–37.
10. "Salman Rushdie: By the Book," *New York Times*, September 17, 2015.
11. Richard Wright, *Native Son* (New York: Harper & Brothers, 1940), 441.
12. Wright, *Native Son*, 440.
13. Wright, *Native Son*, 429.
14. Wright, *Native Son*, 454.

15. Baldwin, *Notes of a Native Son,* 22.

16. Adam Bradley, "Surreal Encounters in Ralph Ellison's 'Invisible Man,'" *New York Times Style Magazine,* June 3, 2021.

17. Frantz Fanon, *Black Skin, White Masks,* trans. Richard Philcox (New York: Grove Press, 2007), 206.

18. Fanon, *Black Skin, White Masks,* 206.

19. Layli Long Soldier, *Whereas* (Minneapolis: Graywolf Press, 2017), 57.

20. Gilles Deleuze and Félix Guattari, *Kafka: Toward a Minor Literature,* trans. Dana Polan (Minneapolis: University of Minnesota Press, 1986), 18.

21. Deleuze and Guattari, *Kafka: Toward a Minor Literature,* 19.

22. Long Soldier, *Whereas,* 74.

23. "Carter: 'Nothing but Sympathy for Families' of MIAs," *Washington Post,* March 24, 1977.

24. Long Soldier, *Whereas,* 92.

25. Mai Der Vang, *Yellow Rain: Poems* (Minneapolis: Graywolf Press, 2021), 5.

26. Vang, *Yellow Rain,* 17.

27. Vang, *Yellow Rain,* 58.

28. Vang, *Yellow Rain,* 59.

29. Vang, "Composition 3," *Yellow Rain,* 109.

30. Hoang Thi Hue, Tuangtip Klinbubpa-Neff, and Thao Do Phuong, "Novels of Vaddey Ratner and Viet Thanh Nguyen—Unpacking Trauma Language, Facing Ghosts, and Killing Shadows," *Humanities and Social Sciences Communications* 118 (2023): 1–6, https://doi.org/10.1057/s41599-023-01587-0.

6. ON THE JOY OF OTHERNESS

1. Andrew Marvell, "To His Coy Mistress," Poetry Foundation, https://www.poetryfoundation.org/poems/44688/to-his-coy-mistress.

2. Fernando Pessoa, *The Book of Disquiet* (London: Penguin Classics, 2002), 48.

3. Italo Calvino, *Six Memos for the Next Millennium* (Cambridge, MA: Harvard University Press, 1988), 8.

4. Calvino, *Six Memos for the Next Millennium,* 14.

5. Thích Nhất Hạnh, *Fragrant Palm Leaves: Journals, 1962–1966* (Berkeley: Parallax Press, 1998), 29.

6. Thích Nhất Hạnh, *Fragrant Palm Leaves,* 99.

7. Thích Nhất Hạnh, *Fragrant Palm Leaves,* 100.

8. Edward P. Jones, *Lost in the City* (New York: Harper Collins, 2009), 8.

9. Jones, *Lost in the City,* 6.

10. Jones, *Lost in the City,* 3.

11. Jones, *Lost in the City,* 11.

12. Jones, *Lost in the City,* 26.

13. Jones, *Lost in the City,* 1.

14. Edwidge Danticat, *Create Dangerously: The Immigrant Artist at Work* (New York: Knopf Doubleday, 2011), 33.

15. Jorge Luis Borges, *This Craft of Verse* (Cambridge, MA: Harvard University Press, 2002), 99.

16. Theodore Roethke, "Words for the Wind," in *The Collected Poems of Theodore Roethke* (New York: Knopf Doubleday, 2011), 121.

17. Fernando Pessoa, *The Book of Disquiet,* trans. Margaret Jull Kosta (London: Serpent's Tail, 1991), 14.

18. Pessoa, *The Book of Disquiet,* 8.

19. Pessoa, *The Book of Disquiet,* 185.

20. Sian Cain, "Maryse Condé, Guadeloupean 'Grand Storyteller' Dies Aged 90," *The Guardian,* April 2, 2024.

21. Emmanuel Levinas, *Totality and Infinity: An Essay on Exteriority,* trans. Alphonso Lingis (Pittsburgh: Duquesne University Press, 1969), 23–47.

22. Derek Walcott, *Collected Poems, 1948–1984* (New York: Farrar, Straus and Giroux, 1986), 346.

23. Ralph Ellison, National Book Awards. Acceptance speech. Box-folder 9:9, "Acceptance Speeches 1959," National Book Foundation archives. Ellison won in 1953, but his speech is catalogued in 1959.

24. Richard Wilbur, National Book Awards ceremony, New York, NY, March 12, 1957. Acceptance speech. Box-folder 9:7, "Acceptance Speeches 1957," National Book Foundation archives.

25. Wilbur, NBA acceptance speech, 1957.

26. William Shakespeare, *The Complete Works of Shakespeare,* ed. W. J. Craig (London: Humphrey Milford, Oxford University Press, 1924), V.v.24, 26–28.

27. Roethke, *The Collected Poems of Theodore Roethke,* 120.

BIBLIOGRAPHY

Achebe, Chinua. *Home and Exile*. New York: Oxford University Press, 2000.

Agamben, Giorgio. *Homo Sacer: Sovereign Power and Bare Life*. Translated by Daniel Heller-Roazen. Redwood City, CA: Stanford University Press, 1998.

Anzaldúa, Gloria. *Borderlands / La Frontera: The New Mestiza*. San Francisco: Aunt Lute Books, 1987.

Arnold, Matthew. *Culture and Anarchy: An Essay in Political and Social Criticism*. London: Smith, Elder, 1889.

Baldwin, James. *Notes of a Native Son*. Boston: Beacon Press, 1955.

Boochani, Behrouz. *No Friend But the Mountains: Writing from Manus Prison*. Translated by Omid Tofighian. London: Picador Australia, 2018.

Borges, Jorge Luis. *This Craft of Verse*. Cambridge, MA: Harvard University Press, 2002.

Bourdieu, Pierre. *The Field of Cultural Production*. New York: Columbia University Press, 1993.

Cain, Sian. "Maryse Condé, Guadeloupean 'Grand Storyteller' Dies Aged 90." *The Guardian,* April 2, 2024. https://www.theguardian.com/books/2024/apr/02/maryse-conde-guadelopean-grand -storyteller-dies-aged-90

Calvino, Italo. *Six Memos for the Next Millennium*. Cambridge, MA: Harvard University Press, 1988.

Carew, Jan. "Going Beyond the Clichés." *New York Times,* September 22, 1974. https://www.nytimes .com/1974/09/22/archives/an-anthology-of-asianamerican-writers-edited-by-jeffery-chan-frank. html.

Cary, Joyce. *Power in Men*. London: Nicholson & Watson / Liberal Book Club, 1939.

"Carter: 'Nothing but Sympathy for Families' of MIAs." *Washington Post,* March 24, 1977. https://www .washingtonpost.com/archive/politics/1977/03/25/carter-nothing-but-sympathy-for-families-of -mias/dbfe5ba5-970b-473a-9f8e-9c5cf2a15637/.

Césaire, Aimé. *A Tempest*. Translated by Richard Miller. New York: UBU Repertory Theater, 1992.

Cha, Theresa Hak Kyung. *Dictee*. Berkeley: University of California Press, 2001.

Chen, Ken. "I Was Ostensibly Searching for My Father, But." Poetry Foundation, April 14, 2016. https://www.poetryfoundation.org/harriet-books/2016/04/i-was-ostensibly-searching-for-my -father-but.

Ch'ien, Evelyn Nien-Ming. *Weird English*. Cambridge, MA: Harvard University Press, 2005.

Chin, Frank, Jeffrey Paul Chan, Lawson Fusao Inada, and Shawn Wong, eds. *Aiiieeeee! An Anthology of Asian-American Writers*. Washington, DC: Howard University Press, 1974.

Chotiner, Isaac. "The Brutal Conditions Facing Palestinian Prisoners." *New Yorker*. March 21, 2024. https://www.newyorker.com/news/q-and-a/the-brutal-conditions-facing-palestinian-prisoners.

Conrad, Joseph. *Heart of Darkness*. Cambridge: Cambridge University Press, 2018.

Coppola, Francis, dir. *Apocalypse Now*. Omni Zoetrope, 1979.

Danticat, Edwidge. *Create Dangerously: The Immigrant Artist at Work*. New York: Knopf Doubleday, 2011.

Darwish, Mahmoud. *Memory for Forgetfulness: August, Beirut, 1982*. Translated by Ibrahim Muhawi. Berkeley: University of California Press, 1995.

Deleuze, Gilles and Félix Guattari. *Kafka: Toward a Minor Literature*. Translated by Dana Polan. Minneapolis: University of Minnesota Press, 1986.

Derrida, Jacques. *Monolingualism of the Other: or, The Prosthesis of Origin*. Translated by Patrick Mensah. Redwood City, CA: Stanford University Press, 1998.

Dickinson, Emily. *The Poems of Emily Dickinson*. Edited by R. W. Franklin. vol. 1. Cambridge, MA: Belknap Press of Harvard University Press, 1998.

Ellison, Ralph. *Invisible Man*. New York: Random House, 1952.

Ellison, Ralph. National Book Awards ceremony, New York, NY, 1953. Acceptance speech.

Everett, Percival. *Erasure*. Lebanon, NH: University Press of New England, 2001.

Fanon, Frantz. *Black Skin, White Masks*. Translated by Richard Philcox. New York: Grove Atlantic, 2008.

Fanon, Frantz. *The Wretched of the Earth*. Translated by Richard Philcox. New York: Grove Atlantic, 2007.

Fitzgerald, F. Scott. *The Great Gatsby*. New York: Charles Scribner's Sons, 1925.

Faulkner, William. *The Sound and the Fury*. New York: Penguin Random House, 1929.

Gordimer, Nadine. *Writing and Being*. Cambridge, MA: Harvard University Press, 1995.

Hoang Thi Hue, Tuangtip Klinbubpa-Neff, and Thao Do Phuong. "Novels of Vaddey Ratner and Viet Thanh Nguyen—Unpacking Trauma Language, Facing Ghosts, and Killing Shadows." *Humanities and Social Sciences Communications* 10, no. 118 (2023): 1–6. https://doi.org/10.1057/s41599-023-01587-0.

Homer. *The Odyssey*. Translated by A. T. Murray. Revised by George E. Dimock. 2 vols. Loeb Classical Library 104, 105. Cambridge, MA: Harvard University Press, 1919.

Hurston, Zora Neale. *How It Feels to Be Colored Me*. New York: Open Road Media, 2024.

Jewett, Sarah Orne. *The Country of the Pointed Firs*. Boston: Houghton Mifflin, 1896.

Jin, Ha. *The Writer as Migrant*. Chicago: University of Chicago Press, 2008.

Jones, Edward P. *Lost in the City*. New York: Harper Collins, 2009.

Jones, Edward P. *The Known World*. New York: Amistad Press, 2003.

Joyce, James. *Ulysses*. Paris: Shakespeare and Company, 1922.

Kingston, Maxine Hong. *The Woman Warrior*. New York: Knopf, 1976.

Kumar, Amitava. *Bombay, London, New York*. London: Routledge, 2002, repr., 2012.

Lahiri, Jhumpa. "The Third and Final Continent." In *Interpreter of Maladies,* 173–198. Boston: Houghton Mifflin, 1999.

Levinas, Emmanuel. *Totality and Infinity: An Essay on Exteriority*. Translated by Alphonso Lingis. Pittsburgh: Duquesne University Press, 1969.

Long Soldier, Layli. *Whereas*. Minneapolis: Graywolf Press, 2017.

Marx, Karl, and Frederich Engels. *The Communist Manifesto*. London: Workers' Educational Association, 1848.

Melville, Herman. *Moby-Dick*. Boston: Houghton Mifflin, 1955.

Milosz, Czeslaw. *The Witness of Poetry*. Cambridge, MA: Harvard University Press, 1983.

Morrison, Toni. *The Origin of Others*. Cambridge, MA: Harvard University Press, 2017.

Murakami, Haruki. *Sputnik Sweetheart*. Translated by Philip Gabriel. New York: Knopf Doubleday, 2002.

Murakami, Haruki. *What I Talk About When I Talk About Running*. Translated by Philip Gabriel. New York: Knopf Doubleday, 2008.

Naipaul, V. S. *The Mimic Men*. London: Penguin Books, 1969.

Nguyen, Viet Thanh. *A Man of Two Faces*. New York: Grove Press, 2023.

Nguyen, Viet Thanh. *Nothing Ever Dies: Vietnam and the Memory of War*. Cambridge, MA: Harvard University Press, 2017.

Nguyen, Viet Thanh. *The Committed*. New York: Grove Press, 2021.

Nguyen, Viet Thanh. *The Sympathizer*. New York: Grove Press, 2015.

Nguyen, Viet Thanh. "War Years." In *The Refugees*, 49–72. New York: Grove Press, 2017.

Otsuka, Julie. *The Buddha in the Attic*. New York: Knopf, 2011.

Oz, Amos. *Fima*. Boston: Mariner Books, 1994.

Panh, Rithy. *The Elimination*. New York: Other Press, 2013.

Pessoa, Fernando. *The Book of Disquiet*. Translated by Margaret Jull Costa. London: Serpent's Tail, 1991.

Phi, Bao. *Sông I Sing*. Minneapolis: Coffee House Press, 2011.

Plath, Sylvia. *The Bell Jar*. Portsmouth, NH: Heinemann, 1963.

Rabee, Osama Abu. "Palestinian Detainees Say They Faced Abuse in Israeli Jails." *Reuters*, June 12, 2024. https://www.reuters.com/world/middle-east/palestinian-detainees-say-they-faced-abuse -israeli-jails-2024-06-12/.

Rimbaud, Arthur. *Correspondance inédite (1870–1875) d'Arthur Rimbaud*. Edited and with an introduction by Roger Gilbert-Lecomte. Paris: Éditions des cahiers libres, 1929.

Roethke, Theodore. *The Collected Poems of Theodore Roethke*. New York: Knopf Doubleday, 2011.

Roy, Arundhati. "Peace & the New Corporate Liberation Theology." City of Sydney Peace Prize Lecture, Sydney, Australia, November 2004.

Rushdie, Salman. *Imaginary Homelands: Essays and Criticism 1981–1991*. London: Penguin, 1992.

Rushdie, Salman. *The Satanic Verses*. New York: Viking Penguin, 1988.

Said, Edward W. *Orientalism*. New York: Pantheon Books, 1978.

Said, Edward W. *Out of Place*. London: Granta Publications, 2013.

Said, Edward W. *Reflections on Exile and Other Essays*. Cambridge, MA: Harvard University Press, 2002.

"Salman Rushdie." *New York Times*, September 17, 2015. https://www.nytimes.com/2015/09/20/books /review/salman-rushdie-by-the-book.html.

Shakespeare, William. *The Complete Works of Shakespeare*. Edited, with a glossary, by W. J. Craig. London: Humphrey Milford, Oxford University Press, 1924.

Sharif, Solmaz. *Look*. Minneapolis: Graywolf Press, 2016.

So, Anthony Veasna. *Afterparties*. New York: Harper Collins, 2021.

Thích Nhất Hạnh. *Fragrant Palm Leaves: Journals, 1962–1966*. Berkeley: Parallax Press, 1998.

Vang, Mai Der. *Yellow Rain: Poems*. Minneapolis: Graywolf Press, 2021.

Walker, Alice. *The Color Purple*. New York: Harcourt Brace Jovanovich, 1982.

Weir, Peter, dir. *Dead Poets Society*. Walt Disney Studios Motion Pictures, 1989.

Wilbur, Richard. National Book Awards ceremony, New York, NY, 1957. Acceptance speech.

Williams, William Carlos. *In the American Grain*. New York: Albert & Charles Boni, 1925.

Wright, Richard. *Native Son*. New York: Harper & Brothers, 1940.

ACKNOWLEDGMENTS

These lectures would not have been possible without the work of the committee that invited me to deliver them: Jonathan Bolton, Glenda Carpio, Robin Kelsey, Jesse McCarthy, Melissa McCormick, Mariano Siskind, and Paul Yoon. I am grateful for their efforts, and for the honor of the invitation.

The lectures were hosted by Harvard's Mahindra Humanities Center, and I am deeply appreciative of the staff who ensured that my visits were always marked by hospitality, generosity, and efficiency: Steven Biel, Bruno Carvalho, Suzannah Clark, and Mary MacKinnon.

It was a pleasure to turn these lectures into a book with Harvard University Press and to work with editorial director Sharmila Sen, editorial associate Samantha Mateo, and publicist Amanda Ice, all of whom have been unflagging in their support. Working on these lectures was made much easier with the help of Titi Nguyen and Kathleen Hoang, who assisted with the notes and copyediting.

These lectures also became better thanks to the writers and scholars who responded to them at Harvard: Min Song, Laila Lalami, Jeff Chang, Ken Chen, Mai Der Vang, and Gina Apostol. I owe them the deepest of debts for their time and insight, while claiming all the limits and flaws of these lectures as my own.

Finally, these lectures draw from the lives of my parents, Joseph and Linda Nguyen, my brother, Tung Nguyen, and my sister, Nguyễn Thị Thanh Hương. I evoke my children, Ellison and Simone, as well. They have all shaped me for the better through their love and inspiration, as has my partner, Lan Duong, the first and the last of my readers.

INDEX

academia, 5, 21
Achebe, Chinua, 15
Adam and Eve story, 64
afterlife, 61, 76, 90
Afterparties (So), 12–13, 20
Agamben, Giorgio, 8
Aiiieeeee! An Anthology of Asian-American Writers (Chin et al.), 43
Algeria, 19, 82
Algerian revolution, 82, 83
alienation, 1, 18–19, 54, 77, 82
American Dream, 15, 26, 35
American empire, 82, 83–84
American history, 28
Americans, 28, 44
Anglo-Saxon literature, 40–41
anti-Asian racism, 45–47, 50–52
anti-Asian violence, 34, 42, 46, 48, 51
anticolonialism, 30–31
antigovernment protests, 69
antisemitism, 45, 50
antiwar movement, against Israel, 41–42
Antunes, António Lobo, 65
Anzaldúa, Gloria, 66–67, 69
Apocalypse Now, 14–16, 18
Arabs, 47, 53, 54, 55
Armstrong, Neil, 60
Arnold, Matthew, 76
art / arts, 10, 11, 12, 75
Asia, 42. See also *specific countries*

Asian American literature, 30, 40–45, 48–49, 51
Asian Americans, 20, 30, 33, 34, 40–53, 56
Asian Pacific Psychiatric Ward, 35–37, 38, 39
Australia, 69–72
authenticity, 100
authors. *See* writers

Baldwin, James, 78–83
Bandung Conference, 82
"bare life," 8, 10
being minor, 73–90
being / nonbeing, 10–11, 96
belief, 10–11
Bellow, Saul, 77
Bible, 64, 75
Black communities, 98–99
Black Panthers, 83
Black Skin, White Masks (Fanon), 82–83
Black writers, 102. *See also specific writers*
Blue Dragon White Tiger (Đinh), 29
body-mind duality, 9–10
bohemian, 11, 18
Boochani, Behrouz, 69–72
The Book of Disquiet (Pessoa), 101
books, 27, 29
Borderlands / La Frontera (Anzaldúa), 66–67, 69
borders: concept of, 71; crossing, 57–72; national, 66–67; US-Mexico, 66–67
Borges, Jorge Luis, 6, 100, 101
Bourdieu, Pierre, 10–11

bourgeoisie, 11
"burden of representation," 19
burial, 61
Byron, Lord, 76

Calvino, Italo, 6, 92
Cambodian genocide, 12–13
canonical literature, 14, 20, 30, 75–77
capacious grief, 23
capital, 12
capitalism, 7, 10, 12, 21, 22, 50–51, 61, 95
Carter, Jimmy, 85
Cary, Joyce, 15
Cather, Willa, 78
Catholicism, 7, 10, 61, 74–75, 95
Césaire, Aimé, 17–19
Cha, Theresa, 67–69
Chan, Jeffrey Paul, 43, 47
Chen, Ken, 62–63
childbirth, 94–95
children, 93, 99–100
Chin, Frank, 43
Chinese, 46, 47, 48, 49, 51
Chinese Americans, 45–48
"The Chinese in Haifa" (Chan), 43–47, 52–54
class, 12
classical music, 9
Cold War, 67
collective identity, 41
collective voices, 34
colonialism, 10, 12, 17, 32, 47, 52, 53
colonization, 35, 38, 42, 50–51, 54, 82–83
The Committed (Nguyen), 18, 64
communism, 7, 15, 57, 96, 104
Condé, Maryse, 102
Conrad, Joseph, 14, 51
Coppola, Francis Ford, 14
This Craft of Verse (Borges), 100
creativity, 93, 95–96
cultural production, 11
culture, 7, 10, 12, 19, 41, 43, 74, 76, 97
Culture and Anarchy (Arnold), 76
cummings, e. e., 5

Danticat, Edwidge, 100
Darwish, Mahmoud, 53–54
Dead White Male literature, 75–76

death, 61–63, 76, 96
decolonization, 30–31
Defoe, Daniel, 70
Deleuze, Gilles, 77, 78, 82, 84
Derrida, Jacques, 19–20, 92
destruction, 7–8
Dickinson, Emily, 77–78, 79
Dictee (Cha), 67–69
Dĩnh, Trân Văn, 29
discipline, 97
domestic violence, 73
double consciousness, 33–34
duality, 3, 17–18
Du Bois, W. E. B., 33

East Asians, 52
economic value, 11
education, 74–75
The Elimination (Panh), 12
Ellison, Ralph, 82, 102
empire, 10, 83–90
Engels, Friedrich, 75
English language, 29–30
enslavement, 12
entrepreneurs, 95
epics, 64
equity, 52
Erasure (Everett), 22–23
Everett, Percival, 22–23
Evers, Medgar, 83
exiles, 8, 54, 60, 61, 64, 70
expansive solidarity, 44, 49–50, 52, 54–56, 80

fables, 64
family, 66, 67
family cleaving, 98–99
Fanon, Frantz, 82–83
fascism, 80
father: background of, 57; border crossings by,
    57–58, 72; death of, 61; as refugee, 60–61;
    religion of, 96, 97; sister's visit to, 105–106;
    son and, 74; underestimation of, 97
fatherhood, 93
Faulkner, William, 75
Filipinos, 48, 51
Fima (Oz), 55
Fitzgerald, F. Scott, 32